SCRAMBLES IN THE DARK PEAK

EASY SUMMER SCRAMBLES AND WINTER CLIMBS

by
Tom Corker and Terry Sleaford

CICERONE

2 POLICE SQUARE, MILNTHORPE, CUMBRIA LA7 7PY
www.cicerone.co.uk

Printed by KHL Printing, Singapore.
A catalogue record for this book is available from the British Library.
All photographs are by the authors unless otherwise stated.

o͞s Ordnance Survey® This product includes mapping data licensed from Ordnance Survey® with the permission of the Controller of Her Majesty's Stationery Office. © Crown copyright 2012. All rights reserved. Licence number PU100012932

Acknowledgements

This guidebook has had a very long gestation period involving many trips into the Peak District. Our heartfelt thanks must therefore go in no small measure to our wives Claire and Eileen, who have patiently supported us whilst we were out having fun. We would like to thank Claire Corker for typing the original manuscript. Photography has been greatly enhanced by the assistance and guidance of Chris Sleaford. Others have provided reassurance and encouragement over the years, in particular John Hammond, Gordon Allan and members of the Castle Mountaineering Club, especially Alison Williams and Marian Birkett. We would also like to thank the staff at Cicerone who have crafted such a professional book from our endeavours.

Advice to Readers

While every effort is made by our authors to ensure the accuracy of guidebooks as they go to print, changes can occur during the lifetime of an edition. If we know of any, there will be an Updates tab on this book's page on the Cicerone website (www.cicerone.co.uk), so please check before planning your trip. We also advise that you check information about such things as transport, accommodation and shops locally. Even rights of way can be altered over time. We are always grateful for information about any discrepancies between a guidebook and the facts on the ground, sent by email to info@cicerone.co.uk or by post to Cicerone, 2 Police Square, Milnthorpe LA7 7PY, United Kingdom.

Front cover: Scrambling in Crowden Clough (Route 34)

CONTENTS

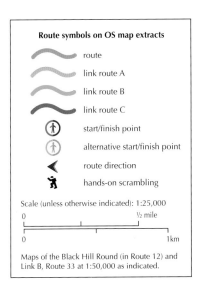

Route symbols on OS map extracts

route

link route A

link route B

link route C

start/finish point

alternative start/finish point

route direction

hands-on scrambling

Scale (unless otherwise indicated): 1:25,000

0   ½ mile

0   1km

Maps of the Black Hill Round (in Route 12) and
Link B, Route 33 at 1:50,000 as indicated.

Warning: Scrambling can be dangerous

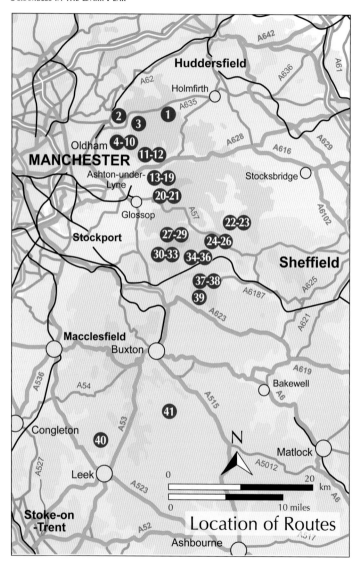

Location of Routes

PREFACE

There are many guides to the Peak District, covering everything from gentle strolls to long-distance walks, family cycle paths to mountain-bike trails, climbing rocks to descending cave systems. Some are particularly specialised and, for example, aircraft crash sites, old railway lines, even trig points have their devotees. This latest addition to the list of such guidebooks is (we believe) the first to focus specifically on scrambling in the Peak District, and the Dark Peak in particular. It is aimed at the more adventurous walker who might wish to add a little more 'spice' to their outings, and also those with some rock-climbing experience who may be looking for something away from the mainstream crags while retaining some element of 'hands-on' contact with the rock.

Tom Corker and Terry Sleaford, 2011

The large slab on the Upper Tier Ridge on The Roaches skyline (Route 40)

INTRODUCTION

The Peak District was designated the UK's first National Park in 1951 and covers an area of more than 1400 square kilometres. It forms the southern end of the Pennines and has long been a magnet for outdoor types, being within easy reach of Manchester, Sheffield, Nottingham and Derby. It is estimated that over ten million visitors a year come to the Park for a variety of reasons, one of the main ones being to walk through the limestone dales in the south (the White Peak) or on the more rugged gritstone moorland in the north (the Dark Peak).

Walking has always been popular here and there are footpaths criss-crossing the whole area but, while visitors to the Dark Peak moors make full use of these to reach their goals, not everyone will be aware of the possibilities that exist to add a little more interest and excitement to their day out. At first glance, opportunities for the more adventurous to get 'hands on' with the rock appear limited to the climbers' crags, but well-known scrambles do exist (Wildboar Clough and the Wilderness Gullies, for example). On closer acquaintance many other opportunities present themselves and by linking some of these together, with a moorland walk in between, it is possible to extend the joys of the hands-on experience into a longer day.

The aim of this guidebook is to highlight and gather together these alternative routes in the hope that others will derive as much pleasure from them as we have over the years. It should certainly provide food for thought for anyone looking for a change from the well-trodden paths that lead onto the tops. Such readers will find these routes truly rewarding. On a good day, in dry sunny weather, the careful placing of hands and feet on clean, water-washed gritstone, while climbing through unique scenery, takes a lot of beating.

At the same time, under good winter conditions of ice and snow, most of the routes can offer the same uplifting experience and a straightforward ascent. Some routes, however, are more serious outings in winter and the general warnings given below and more specifically in the route descriptions should be heeded.

SCRAMBLING IN THE DARK PEAK

So, is there really any scrambling in the Peak District? Well, if the definition of a scramble is that the use of hands is necessary to complete an ascent, then the answer is a definite 'yes'! As mentioned above, there are some well-known and classic scrambling routes in the Dark Peak, but note that this is not Snowdonia or the

*The wide chimney in the top section of Nether Red Brook (Route 27)
(Photograph: Chris Sleaford)*

Lake District and readers should not expect to be gambolling along high airy ridges or enjoying the thrills of a multi-pitched ascent (although there are one or two of these). There may also be a need to adopt a 'blinkered' approach at times, as some lines are close to a path or bordered by grassy slopes; but if this is the umpteenth time that you have been in a particular area, always following the same path, then these alternatives are well worth a try.

Once engaged with the pleasure of using your hands to move easily over sun-warmed rock, or maybe kicking steps up a snow-filled gully in winter, ascents onto the moors may become a little more interesting and enjoyable. At the same time, these routes provide an opportunity to learn or practise the basic skills that will prove useful in the more serious setting of the big mountains.

WARNINGS AND PRECAUTIONS

The activities described in this guidebook are potentially dangerous. The range of difficulty on offer is very wide and users should have attained a suitable level of skill and experience to enable the chosen route to be completed in a safe and enjoyable manner. Conditions and circumstances will change as the natural processes of nature take a hand, and the best line of ascent for any given route may change over time.

You must decide what is best under the prevailing conditions and take all due precautions and routes should only be attempted in reasonably good conditions.

It is good practice to check the weather forecast before venturing out and prepare accordingly, and you should always let someone know your plans for the day.

Should an emergency arise while out on the moors, dial 999 or 112 and ask for Police and then Mountain Rescue. There is also a text message service available for which you need to pre-register which is straightforward to use and may work where signal strength is weak. Details are available from the Mountain Rescue contacts given in Appendix C.

Newcomers should try routes at Grade 1 at first to see how they get on before trying the harder ones.

However, even here greasy and/or loose rock may be encountered, and a slip could have serious consequences. Moving safely in such conditions requires practice to develop confidence; the following tips may help.

- Before committing to a slippery foothold get a good handhold.
- Squeeze a boot between rocks or push it into corners or to the back of flat ledges.
- Stand on sharp edges or in cracks to give the sole of the boot a chance to bite.
- The use of a knee is sometimes the best option!

If in any doubt, do not use suspect holds; try to find another way over or around the obstacle, or back off altogether and escape to easier

Around halfway up Fair Book Gully (Route 26) (Photograph: Chris Sleaford)

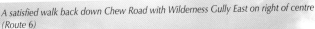

A satisfied walk back down Chew Road with Wilderness Gully East on right of centre (Route 6)

ground (this is not always possible on routes of Grade 2 and above). Such routes may also require the use of a rope in places and it is recommended that one be carried either to protect the party from the beginning or simply to give confidence as a back-up should difficulties arise.

More experienced users may well prefer to go solo and will not feel the same sense of danger as on higher mountain scrambles. However, a fall in an isolated clough or ravine, where others are unlikely to pass by regularly, could have serious consequences. Add the fact that some of the routes are in relatively remote locations, and the dangers inherent in soloing become obvious.

Additional precautions for winter conditions

Under winter conditions everything changes dramatically, especially during a hard winter. The use of crampons and ice axes will probably be necessary, so think ahead and go out fully prepared. Modern mountaineering axes with curved picks will usually suffice, as will crampons intended for general mountaineering use when properly fitted onto suitable boots. If in doubt, specialist climbing equipment shops can offer sound advice.

Moving over snow and ice wearing crampons needs practice, even if only as a refresher, and easy Peak District scrambles are excellent for this purpose (better to trip over your

Back Tor in a light dusting of snow (Route 37)

crampons here than on some higher and more unforgiving mountain slope or ridge!). Many of the routes described can be climbed at a reasonable standard in snowy, verglassed, or even full ice conditions. It is a truly variable feast and what might be encountered on any given day cannot be fully predicted. Small ice pitches often form after a relatively short period of frost (snow or no snow) especially in the north-facing cloughs. Some longer ice pitches can also form, and some may wish to practise their winter skills by climbing them. These same pitches can usually be top-roped and equipment could be shared to enable everyone in the party to have a go. Beginners should start on the easier routes to see how it goes and to build up their confidence.

After very heavy snowfall, in warmer or wet conditions, serious avalanches have been known to occur, as highlighted by the deaths of Graham West and Michael Roberts, both experienced mountaineers, while climbing in Wilderness Gully in January 1963. Deaths have occurred in other areas too, Dovestones Central Gully being one such place. The advice therefore, is to **avoid steeper locations immediately after very heavy snowfall or in wet, thawing conditions**.

The shale cliffs of Mam Tor, Back Tor and Alport Castles are really included only for the adrenalin junkies. They should be approached **only after snow and a prolonged period of frost** and are **not recommended** as ascents at any other time of year.

EQUIPMENT

Most people will have their own ideas about this, but for the less experienced the following suggestions may be useful. A compass and the relevant map should always be taken, as should some sort of torch for the winter months. Be aware that winter ascents will require specialist equipment and should not be attempted without it and the knowledge of how to use it (see 'Additional precautions for winter conditions' above).

Clothing Normal hill-walking clothing is generally suitable. Most people have personal preferences regarding outfits for the different seasons, but conditions can change dramatically and suddenly at any time of year, so be prepared. In winter especially, conditions on the moors of the Dark Peak can be 'arctic' so always ensure you have adequate warm clothing, gloves or mittens (and spares), a hat and waterproofs (ideally of the breathable type).

Footwear Lightweight walking boots (ideally waterproof) with a firm midsole are ideal for most of the year. To attempt routes in winter, a decent 3/4 season boot suitable for crampon attachment is needed. A full-blown mountain boot isn't necessary, although some may prefer to use them for the steeper ice pitches or as practice for more serious fare elsewhere. All good climbing equipment shops will give sound advice on the choice of boots.

Rope A short (or half-length) 9mm climbing rope is usually satisfactory for the routes in this guidebook, whether

A damp day at Alderman's Rocks (Route 2)

taken as a precautionary measure or to boost confidence. Many people use the thinner 'scrambling' ropes, which can be doubled if required. Whichever rope is chosen, it should always be purchased from a specialist climbing shop – the days of using your mum's washing line are long gone! The use of a rope implies the use of belays and, possibly, the placing of intermediate protection (nuts). A few tape slings, belaying device, and a small selection of medium-sized nuts should suffice. Again, people will have their own preferences.

Helmets These are a sensible precaution on the steeper scrambles, especially those with a rock-climbing grade. A lightweight mountaineering model is a good choice, and wearing one will already have become a habit for those with rock-climbing experience.

Trekking poles On the easier routes, a trekking pole may prove useful in maintaining balance both in ascent and descent. On more difficult sections they can become a hindrance and should be packed away, although some people dangle them from the wrist loop for moves where two hands are needed. They are particularly useful, of course, when crossing streams.

All of the above implies knowledge of such equipment and the ability to use it safely. For the uninitiated, books about climbing techniques and the use of equipment can be found in specialist climbing shops or most large libraries; *The Hillwalker's Guide to Mountaineering* by Terry Adby and Stuart Johnson (Cicerone Press) covers

the essential skills for those moving 'up' from hill walking to scrambling and mountaineering. Even better, experienced friends will be able to show you the basics. Other options would be to enrol on an instruction course or join a local climbing club; the British Mountaineering Council (BMC) in Manchester will be able to provide details of those in your area.

MAPS

The Ordnance Survey 1:25,000 Explorer OL1 (Dark Peak) map covers all the routes except for The Roaches and Chrome and Parkhouse Hills, when the OL24 (White Peak) map will be needed. Please note that place names highlighted in the route descriptions refer to these 1:25,000 maps, sections of which are reproduced in each route. Many of the footpaths mentioned in the text are not shown on the OS maps and can be fairly indistinct in some cases, especially where described as a 'vague path' or 'sheep track'. At other times it will be a case of 'find the best way'. Where given, National Grid references are quoted to six digits only (eg SK 123 456), close enough to enable the feature to be found on the map.

As anyone who has become 'misplaced' on the moors of the Dark Peak knows, it is very easy to get lost in poor visibility. So before this happens, check that you've got the right map and a compass with you and, more importantly, that you know how to use them.

Climbing the slab out of Holme Clough (Route 1)

ABOUT THE ROUTES

All the routes selected for inclusion in this guidebook are within the Peak District National Park, the majority being on gritstone or within the gritstone areas, and most can be done all year round. While some of the routes are classics (Wildboar Clough and the Wilderness Gullies for example), others – such as Torside Gully and Oaken Clough – are less well known but have the potential to achieve classic status with increased use.

The range of difficulty encountered for most of the year ranges from scrambly walks (clambering), to short pitches of rock climbing at up to 'Difficult' standard. A short rope and some equipment could be useful for the latter, and this is mentioned in the route description where relevant. Some routes follow features on rock outcrops that already contain rock climbs recorded in climbers' guidebooks (Alderman's Rocks, Torside Rocks and the area around the Kinder Downfall ravine). Users should note that retreat or escape from such routes may not always be easy.

In the majority of cases, suggestions are given for linking a route to others in the same area to create longer outings while maintaining interest and prolonging the scrambling experience. This will sometimes involve descending a route in order to ascend another. Suggestions for including a circular walk have also been included where it offers interest to extend the day. Be aware that

suitable time allowances should be made when following any of the suggested links, especially in winter when daylight is limited (or if you are parked in a pay-and-display car park!). Always check the description against the map for an assessment of the extra distance involved.

Considering conditions

Many of the routes are based in cloughs on the gritstone bedrock, a very forgiving medium on which to scramble and, therefore, the majority of routes will 'go' in most conditions. However, after heavy rain some routes will be affected by a temporary high level of water flow that may well render them un-climbable for the next 48 hours or so. Once this deluge has passed – and also during a period of lighter rain or even just heavy mist – some of the rock can become green and slippery for a while. Always be prepared to abandon the route if conditions become too difficult as a result.

In winter, under a covering of snow and/or ice, ascents of most routes at standards low in terms of mainstream winter gradings should still be possible, hence their inclusion as a form of scrambling rather than full-blown winter climbs. On the other hand, a few routes will present a serious undertaking in full winter conditions and they are graded accordingly. A few routes for which an ascent is only recommended when hard freezing winter conditions prevail have

Near the top in Wilderness Gully East (Route 6)

also been included, as they are recognised classics at a reasonable standard of difficulty. Remember though, that an ascent of any route under full winter conditions will require ice axes, crampons and usually a rope (and the knowledge of how to use them).

Taking all this into consideration, two or more ascents of the same route, made under different conditions, will present completely different challenges and experiences. What might be encountered is not easy to predict, which just adds to the fun!

Timings
It is hard to give an estimate of the time taken for each route – conditions on the day and personal ability both come into play – but the majority are

intended as half-day outings (up to four hours); adding any of the suggested links will obviously increase the time that should be allowed.

'Height gain'
'Height gain' used in the information box at the beginning of each route description relates to the approximate height gain between **where the scrambling starts and the top of the route**. For the more vertical routes this may seem obvious, but for those routes based in easy-angled cloughs it will inevitably include some walking between scrambling sections, so the height gain quoted here will be spread over the distance from where a streambed is first entered or the first rock step encountered.

19

Easy scrambling in Fair Brook (Route 25)

Route gradings

The convention of numerical grades 1 to 3 has been used (as has the use of 1/2 or 2/3 to indicate borderline cases). **Note** Although the grades in this book compare with those used for the Lake District and Snowdonia in similar guidebooks under good conditions, it is likely that **the grades will feel easier than these high mountain areas in wet and poor conditions** as the gritsone stays grippy even in the wet. The lower exposure of many of the routes also contributes to a less serious feel.

Gritstone is a very different rock on which to scramble – it has very good frictional qualities and can be climbed in almost any conditions – and the use of the numerical grading system here is intended only as a comparative guide to the level of difficulty to be found between routes contained in this guidebook. The use of a rope should be considered for routes of Grade 2 and above, and even experienced scramblers may find this reassuring on Grade 3 routes.

Winter gradings do more closely equate to those in conventional use for winter climbing in the UK, and specialised winter climbing equipment will be required for their safe ascent.

Grade 1 Summer/Grade 1 Winter

Scrambly walks (clambering), short pitches, easy winter climbing.

Grade 2 Summer/Grade 1–2 Winter

Some slightly more technical pitches, longer and steeper, easy summer climbing. Relatively easy winter climbing, depending on the amount of snow and ice present.

Grade 3 Summer/Grade 2–3 Winter

Steeper still and may contain short pitches, or moves, of up to 'Difficult' rock-climbing standards with potentially serious situations. More serious winter climbing.

The conditions encountered throughout the year can vary enormously and may alter a route's subjective grading accordingly. It is hard to compare beautifully water-washed, dry gritstone with the same rock, wet and greasy after rain or under a layer of snow or ice. However, pitches are usually quite short with a good ledge for take-off and holds are usually positive, making ascents in poor conditions more challenging but not necessarily harder in a technical sense. It is often possible to escape to easy ground or to go around difficulties; the choice is left to the individual's judgement. Quite often there will be higher graded routes in the same area than those described in this guide, but these fall outside the scope of the book.

Star rating

This is intended to give an indication as to the quality of the routes described. Lack of a star does not mean the route has no merit. Some routes are marred by sections of grass or loose rock, but could improve with more use and in future be upgraded. The ratings are as follows:

* An interesting route. This may relate in part to the location, the views, interesting features such as waterfalls and pools, as much as to the actual scrambling.

** A good route with nice scrambling and qualities similar to those of a one-star route.

*** An excellent route that may already be an acknowledged classic, or a route that has qualities that could lead to it achieving 'classic' status in the future.

These ratings are naturally subjective at best and depend on individual ideas as to what constitutes a quality route. Personal fitness, prevailing weather conditions and the amount of water in a clough or gully will all have an influence on how good a particular route or day out appears on the day.

ACCESS

The gaining of access rights for the general public to the hills and moors of the Peak District was a long-fought and hard-won battle, some areas only being opened up quite recently as a result of the CROW Act of 2000. Thanks to the efforts of many in the past, 'the right to roam' now applies to much of the moorland in the Dark Peak.

Nevertheless, there are some exceptions; access to the moors may still be temporarily restricted at any time (particularly during the grouse-shooting season), but there will rarely be a problem provided you abide by the notices posted at access points. In Longdendale, on the approaches to Wildboar Clough or Shining Clough, you must stay on the designated access paths until 'open country' is reached.

At the same time, the inclusion of routes in the Winnats Pass and at Mam Tor, Back Tor and Alport Castles, does not automatically imply a right to climb them. They are in sensitive areas and should be respected as such when planning a visit. The approach should be to follow all information, guidelines or warning notices posted at points of access, and to keep up to date by contacting the relevant organisations listed in Appendix C.

CONSERVATION

Conservation and the environment are issues of increasing importance, and ones that all outdoor activities must consider. The whole of the Dark Peak is designated as a Site of Special Scientific Interest and is of international significance. All users have a duty of care under the Wildlife and Countryside Act 1981 and the Countryside Code, which gives the following guidance on the responsibility of the individual:

Not normally a broad sandy footpath, this is the dry bed of the River Kinder en route to Kinder Downfall (Route 34)

- be safe, plan ahead and follow the signs.
- leave gates and property as you find them.
- protect plants and animals and take your litter home.
- keep dogs under close control.
- consider other people.

Many of the routes described in this guidebook involve the use of cloughs and gullies, which are watercourses draining run-off from the peat moorland above and, in some cases, freshwater springs from lower in the geology. Some cloughs take water all year round from top to bottom (for example Holme Clough), while others remain dry for most of the year above the spring line and are only fully wet after very heavy rain or in the winter months.

When following any of these routes it is usually possible to stay close to the line of the main watercourse, thus ensuring that most of the work is done on clean, regularly water-scoured rock where vegetation is at a minimum or, quite often, totally absent.

One notable exception is Oaken Clough in the Crowden area. It has a number of trees along its banks and is generally more verdant than the other cloughs included in this book. Special care should be exercised here to avoid any damage to the trees and surrounding vegetation.

The peat bogs of Kinder, Bleaklow and Black Hill (from which the watercourses flow) store carbon dioxide and it is estimated that the country's peat bogs as a whole currently store ten times our total carbon dioxide emissions. Erosion or other damage results in them leaking this carbon dioxide rather than storing it. Again, estimates put the level of leakage of carbon dioxide from the southern Pennine bogs alone as equivalent to that produced by a town of 50,000 inhabitants.

At the time of writing (2011) a great deal of work is being done by the Moors for the Future partnership to reverse this process by restoring moorland habitats and preventing further erosion. Anyone who has not visited the Bleaklow plateau for a few years would be amazed at the transformation that has taken place since 2003 as a result of reseeding, clough damming and sheep exclusion, among other measures. Similar restoration work began on Kinder Scout in late 2010. Who knows, in the near future Black Hill may need to be renamed Green Hill!

Finally, remember that all the watercourses encountered in this guidebook eventually drain into reservoirs, whose contents are then treated to provide our domestic drinking water. Take care and do not wilfully pollute any of them.

Bird restrictions
In recent years the peregrine falcon has made a return to the Peak District and pairs have been seen nesting at Torside Rocks, Alport Castles, Shining Clough and Laddow Rocks (but not necessarily in all these places every year). Their nesting sites can vary from one year to the next and up-to-date information regarding any restrictions that might be in place can be found by visiting the BMC website. Peregrines enjoy the highest level of legal protection under Schedule 1 of the Wildlife and Countryside Act 1981, which makes it an offence to capture, injure or kill a

Bleaklow Head area – above in 2005 and below in 2011, with the results of reseeding beginning to show

Waterfall in Holme Clough (Route 1)

peregrine or its young, or to damage or destroy its nest or eggs. It is also an offence to intentionally disturb the birds close to their nest sites during the breeding season. Any violation could result in a hefty fine or even a prison sentence. According to the RSPB website, the most sensitive period for peregrines begins around late March, when the birds are laying their eggs, and it can be late June before the chicks are fully fledged.

These birds fly high and make a very distinctive high-pitched shriek, which they repeat over and over again if they feel threatened; if they are nesting nearby and become disturbed, it would be difficult not to be aware of this. Prolonged disturbance could result in them leaving the nest unattended, putting eggs at risk of damage due to cooling, or newly hatched chicks going hungry and potentially

starving to death. It is estimated that less than a third of peregrines reach breeding age, so it seems ridiculous to put their livelihood at further risk for the sake of a little scrambling. Be prepared to back away and go somewhere else, leaving the birds in peace, and return after the period of risk is over.

Another large bird which may be nesting hereabouts is the raven. While this is not a Schedule 1 bird, like all others it is protected by law under the Wildlife and Countryside Act. The most critical period for non-disturbance of these birds is early March to mid-May. For further information about conservation and environmental issues, or the latest details of any restrictions, contact The Peak District National Park Authority, Natural England or The British Mountaineering Council. Website and postal addresses for these organisations are given in Appendix C.

THE CHEW VALLEY AREA

The waterfall and pool (and greasy pole that adds excitement) between Routes 7 and 8 in Chew Brook

This is the most northerly area covered by this guidebook and most interest is located close to Dove Stone Reservoir, to the east of Greenfield on the A635 Greenfield-to-Holmfirth road. The Chew Valley has been popular with rock climbers and walkers for many years and is a delightful place to visit. Dove Stone Reservoir is home to a sailing club and is very popular as a venue for family walks and cycling trips, with a good path going all the way around it. There is a pay-and-display car park and good toilet facilities. For the scrambler, this area contains one of the Peak District's most classic routes, Wilderness Gully East, which was given three stars in the rock-climbers' guidebooks to Chew Valley, at an 'Easy' to 'Moderate' grade – high praise indeed!

The first route described here is, in fact, a bit of an outlier, situated away to the northeast of Chew Valley proper, where the Saddleworth Moors meet the Wessenden Moors at just about the highest point of the A635.

ROUTE 1
Rimmon Pit Clough–Trinnacle–Holme Clough

Start/Finish	Lay-by on A365 on Wessenden Moor, SE 051 063
Height gain	200–225m
Grade and rating	1 (summer and winter) *

Easy-angled scrambling on interesting sections of gritstone bedrock, which is delightful to scramble over in dry conditions. This route takes in two contrasting cloughs and there is a superb photo opportunity on top of a tall rock pinnacle known as The Trinnacle. Holme Clough contains a beautiful little waterfall pitch above a pool. The whole route could be followed in the reverse direction, but is more enjoyable as described.

Approach
Park at the large lay-by on the north side of the A635. This is marked on the map and is where the old alternative Pennine Way path from Black Hill to Marsden crosses the A635. Walk westwards from the car park for a few hundred metres to a locked gate on the south side of the road. A track leads from here down to the ruins of Rimmon Cottage (SE 044 058) where only the walls remain of what today might be called a 'development opportunity'.

Route
Just past the cottage drop down into Rimmon Pit Clough. Follow the line of the main watercourse downstream, keeping to the rock as far as possible (the line taken will vary with prevailing conditions). Lower down, the walls of the clough get higher and begin to close in. A

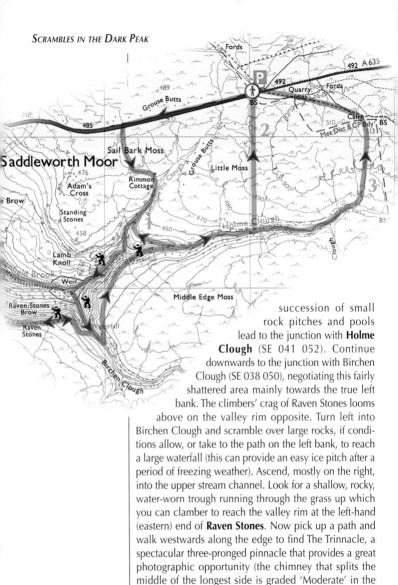

succession of small rock pitches and pools lead to the junction with **Holme Clough** (SE 041 052). Continue downwards to the junction with Birchen Clough (SE 038 050), negotiating this fairly shattered area mainly towards the true left bank. The climbers' crag of Raven Stones looms above on the valley rim opposite. Turn left into Birchen Clough and scramble over large rocks, if conditions allow, or take to the path on the left bank, to reach a large waterfall (this can provide an easy ice pitch after a period of freezing weather). Ascend, mostly on the right, into the upper stream channel. Look for a shallow, rocky, water-worn trough running through the grass up which you can clamber to reach the valley rim at the left-hand (eastern) end of **Raven Stones**. Now pick up a path and walk westwards along the edge to find The Trinnacle, a spectacular three-pronged pinnacle that provides a great photographic opportunity (the chimney that splits the middle of the longest side is graded 'Moderate' in the rock-climbers' guide).

Picture taken, retrace the route eastwards to where the steepness of the slope eases off and pick up a vague path leading diagonally down to the streambed in Birchen Clough. Nearby on the opposite bank is another shallow and rocky, water-worn trough. Ascend this to reach the moor above (Middle Edge Moss) and then head north, aiming for the start of **Holme Clough** near to the waterfall marked on the map (SE 042 052). A steep, rocky, descent leads towards this picturesque waterfall and its pool and the scrambling starts with a short pitch up the left side of the fall. Continue to work up the clough, keeping to the rock as much as possible, until forced out onto a vague path on the left bank.

Options from here are either to head northwest across open moorland back to the upper reaches of Rimmon Pit Clough and ascend this to return to the car park (1), or to continue to follow Holme Clough until, as it begins to narrow, some slabby rocks on the left bank provide an easy scramble to reach the moor above (2). From here, head north over open moorland to return to the car park

The Trinnacle at Raven Stones with Greenfield Reservoir in the background

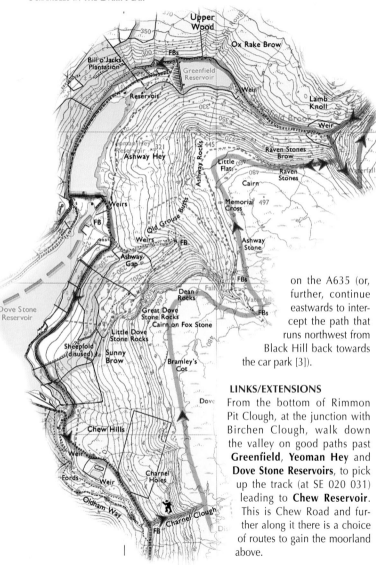

on the A635 (or, further, continue eastwards to intercept the path that runs northwest from Black Hill back towards the car park [3]).

LINKS/EXTENSIONS

From the bottom of Rimmon Pit Clough, at the junction with Birchen Clough, walk down the valley on good paths past **Greenfield**, **Yeoman Hey** and **Dove Stone Reservoirs**, to pick up the track (at SE 020 031) leading to **Chew Reservoir**. This is Chew Road and further along it there is a choice of routes to gain the moorland above.

Link A

Ascend Charnel Clough (Route 4). From the top of Charnel Clough, take the path that leads north along the edge of the moor to Dean Rocks (SE 027 039), then **Ashway Rocks** (SE 029 048) and onwards to **Raven Stones** (SE 036 048) and the Trinnacle. Return to the A635 car park by ascending Rimmon Pit Clough or by following **Holme Clough** and the continuations as described in Route 1.

Link B

Any of the Wilderness Gullies (Routes 5–9). From the top of these routes follow the path along the valley rim eastwards to **Chew Reservoir** and pick up the path leading west along the edge of the moor to the top of Charnel Clough. Continue from here as in Link A.

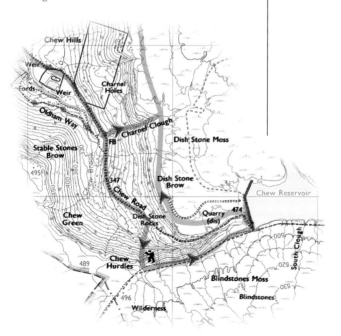

ROUTE 2

Alderman's Rocks

Start/Finish	Binn Green car park, SE 018 044 (or alternatives)
Height gain	10–20m
Grade and rating	2/3 (summer) *

Alderman's Rocks (SE 016 045) and many of the other large boulders strewn around the Chew Valley are said to have been thrown in battle by legendary giants Alphin and Alderman when doing battle for the favours of a water nymph named Rimmon. If the climbing isn't to your liking, the entrance to the 'Fairy Hole', about 50m to the north of the summit, is worth an exploratory look. In truth these are not really scrambles. They actually feel more like lower-grade rock climbs, but they are short and have been included for their wonderful position overlooking the valley and the fact that they lead to an actual summit, of sorts. The rock is excellent and shows signs of much traffic over the years. The use of a rope is recommended if the rock is wet.

Approach

The best option is to park either in Binn Green car park or in the lay-by just south of the entrance to it on the A635. There is a steep path to the rocks immediately across the road from the car park. A less steep approach is available by parking in a lay-by about 500m further north up the road. There is a signpost and stile about 250m further on (SE 018 051) and a path leads from here up towards the rocks on the skyline. The aim is to arrive beneath the large buttress lying below the summit rocks. Work up steep ground to a well-worn ledge below the

Grade 2/3 route at Alderman's Rocks

33

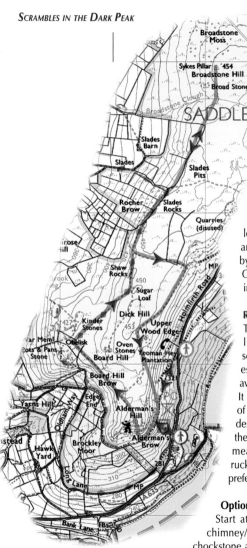

climber's route 'Great Slab', which sits more or less in the middle of the lowest point of the buttress and is bounded on its right by a chimney (Great Slab Chimney, graded 'Difficult' in the climbers' guide).

Routes

There are several suitable lines with considerable scope for variation with an escape onto easy ground available about halfway up. It is suggested that a couple of these lines be completed, descending rocky ground to the west between routes (this means you can leave your rucksack at the bottom if you prefer to go uncluttered).

Option 1 Grade 2/3

Start at the base of an obvious chimney/gully line with a midway chockstone about 4m left (west) of the corner of Great Slab. Climb the chimney to a ledge then either go slightly left up a cracked corner to arrive below a narrow chimney/gully on the left (this has well-worn, stepped holds) or go straight up the corner/cracks on the right. Reach another ledge then, for maximum photographic pose potential, step right onto an exposed nose and climb this easily to the top.

Option 2 Grade 2/3

Climb the chimney as before to the ledge, then work to the right and round the corner over blocks heading for a steep corner. The brave may like to try this, but mere mortals may prefer to traverse delicately to the right from the big block below the corner and then work up left taking in as much rock as possible to the top.

Option 3 Grade 2/3

To the right (east) of the Great Slab are slabby rocks, the lowest having a wide crack in the centre. Work up above this using as much rock as possible to finish in the same place as the previous line, or (better) traverse left on the midway ledge to finish up the chimney/gully of the first route.

Honour satisfied, walk up from the top of the crag to surmount the 'summit rocks'. Choose a line to suit, the most interesting being on the left-hand side going over large blocks to reach a memorial plaque just below the top. Return to the car by reversing the approach path.

From the summit, complete a circular walk to the north, where other 'scrambly' outcrops can be found such as Pots and Pans (SE 010 051), Kinder Stones (SE 011 053), Shaw Rocks (SE 015 056) and Slades Rocks (SE 017 061) on the way to **Broadstone Hill** (SE 021 069). Reverse the route towards Shaw Rocks and pick up the relevant outward path to return to the car park.

ROUTE 3
Dovestone Quarry Central Gully

Start/Finish	Binn Green car park, SE 018 044 (or alternative)
Height gain	80m
Grade and rating	1/2 (winter only)

A long route to the valley rim that takes a line through the middle of the large quarried gritstone buttresses. The Dovestone quarries (SE 025 039) stand high above the northern end of Dove Stone Reservoir and were very popular with rock climbers in the past, although not so much nowadays. In recent years a voluntary access restriction due to peregrines nesting has been in place during the spring, so check for the latest information before making a visit. Due to the loose ground above and the consequent danger of rockfall, this route is recommended for ascent only in good freezing winter conditions and not at any other time of year. On a cautionary note, be aware that a fatal avalanche occurred here in 1980 in deep, wet snow conditions.

Approach

Park in Binn Green car park and follow the path down to and across the **Yeoman Hey Reservoir** dam wall to the gate at the bottom of **Ashway Gap** (SE 023 043). A path leads easily uphill from here alongside the water channel to a footbridge (SE 027 043). Cross the bridge and follow a path gently uphill along the line of a fence (stiles) into the area of the main quarry, where **Central Gully** cuts through the rocks. There is also parking below the dam wall at Dove Stone Reservoir (SE 013 036), which gives a longer walk in,

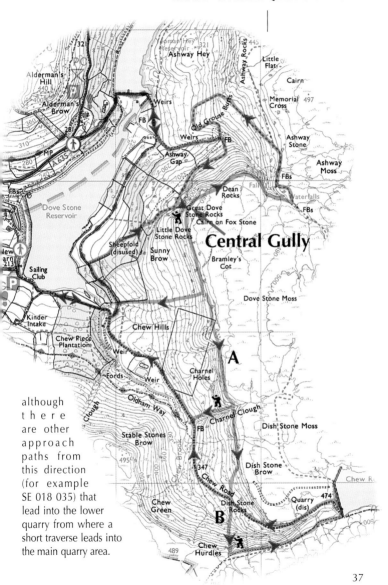

although there are other approach paths from this direction (for example SE 018 035) that lead into the lower quarry from where a short traverse leads into the main quarry area.

Route

Gain the line of the gully and move up towards the narrow section. A short awkward step low down in this narrow part of the gully leads to more straightforward climbing up to the moor edge above. Depending on conditions, a traverse to the left just below the top leads below the rock-climbing crag of Dovestones Edge, where it may be possible to climb an easy gully to the top.

The best options for a descent from here are the easier slopes near **Ashway Stone** to the north (path at SE 031 042) or those near Bramley's Cot (SE 026 035) to the south, depending on which car park was used.

LINKS/EXTENSIONS

Link A

Follow the edge of the moor southwards and descend Charnel Clough (Route 4) to return down Chew Road to the car parks. If parked at Binn Green, it is an easy walk back from here along the reservoir path.

Link B

As above, but walk past the top of Charnel Clough and descend a steep slope near Dish Stone Rocks (SE 029 018) to cross Chew Road and **Chew Brook** to ascend one of the **Wilderness Gullies** (Routes 5–9). Walk eastwards along the edge of the moor to **Chew Reservoir** and return down Chew Road to the car park as for Link A.

ROUTE 4
Charnel Clough

Start/Finish	Car park at Dove Stones Reservoir, SE 013 036
Height gain	120m
Grade and rating	1 (summer and winter) *

This is a bit of a hidden gem that begins (SE 025 024) from the side of Chew Road. The route follows a streambed through a steep-sided clough with a pleasant, easy pitch near the top and an option to climb rocks on the right to gain the valley rim. It can be used as an alternative descent to Chew Road when linked with other routes in this area. After a period of heavy frost, easy ice pitches can form in the upper reaches of the clough (snow or no snow).

Approach

Park at the pay-and-display car park below the dam wall at **Dove Stones Reservoir**. Walk past the sailing clubhouse to the bridge (SE 019 032) over **Chew Brook**. Cross this and turn right to follow the tarmacked track (Chew Road) towards **Chew Reservoir**. After about 1km a gate across the road marks the entrance to Charnel Clough (SE 025 024). ▶

Purists may prefer to follow the path alongside Chew Brook, which starts just before the bridge beyond the clubhouse and rises later to meet Chew Road near the bottom of Charnel Clough (but look out for speeding mountain-bikers!).

Route

Leave the road and enter the clough, moving from the right bank to the left. Follow a vague path on the left bank until you feel like getting involved with the rock. There are a number of short steps, climbed with interest, leading towards a much larger pitch just over halfway up. Climb this to finish via blocks over to the left at the top. In a good winter this pitch gives an interesting, albeit easy, ice climb. Bouldering fans may like to have a go at the enticing slabby boulder on the left bank just after this pitch.

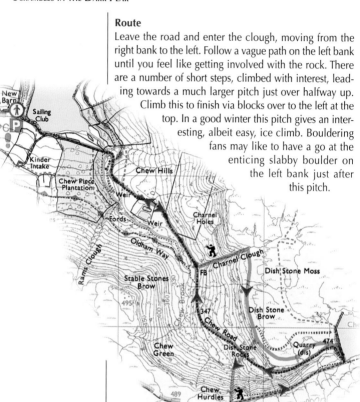

Continue to follow the streambed to the top or, a short distance above, make an exit on the right to climb a series of short gritstone walls high up on the right-hand side of the clough (choosing a line to suit ability). From the top of the clough follow the path along the edge of the moor southwards and on to **Chew Reservoir**. From here descend Chew Road to return to the car park.

The big rock pitch in Charnel Clough

41

Charnel Clough's big rock pitch iced over in winter

LINKS/EXTENSIONS

To prolong the day's enjoyment, make an ascent of one of the Wilderness Gullies (Routes 5–9). Follow the edge of the moor southwards and descend the slope to Chew Road just before reaching Dish Stone Rocks (SE 029 018). The **Wilderness Gullies** are opposite and can now be reached by a further descent from the road to cross **Chew Brook**. From the top of the gullies walk eastwards to Chew Reservoir and descend Chew Road to return to the car park.

THE WILDERNESS GULLIES

This section relates to the steep southern side of the valley enclosing Chew Brook where it turns eastwards towards Chew Reservoir. These slopes are north facing and after a good period of frosty weather ice forms in the gullies, snow or no snow. Walking up Chew Road from the bottom of Charnel Clough, several gully lines begin to appear on the slopes to the south. The first two have been ignored for this guidebook, as they contain little in the way of continuous rock. Further along, a series of rock buttresses, Chew Hurdles (SE 028 016), can be seen just below the skyline and it is here where most interest lies. Two deep gullies (Routes 5 and 6) split the buttresses and these are the best and most obvious lines, whereas the other three described (Routes 7–9) are most clearly seen when standing opposite them on Chew Road. The routes are described from right to left, in the order reached when walking up Chew Road (or following the Chew Brook streambed as in Route 10).

One note of caution regarding winter ascents: a fatal avalanche, which resulted in the deaths of two experienced climbers, occurred here in 1963 following heavy snowfall.

ROUTE 5
Wilderness Gully West

Start/Finish	Car park at Dove Stones Reservoir, SE 013 036
Height gain	130m
Grade and rating	1 (summer and winter) *

The first deep gully line falling from the rock buttresses on the right of Chew Road: a long scramble over blocks and rock slabs, the line taken depending on prevailing conditions. Not quite as good as its neighbour (Route 6), but well worth an ascent. It leads from the banks of Chew Brook right up to the valley rim and could be used, with care, as a descent. After prolonged frost, easy-angled ice can form for a long way up this route.

Approach

View over Dove Stone Reservoir. The Wilderness gullies are in the far distance

As for Charnel Clough (Route 4), but go through the gate and follow Chew Road round to the left until it is possible to drop down the slope to **Chew Brook**. A vague path leads diagonally down to the stream where a suitable crossing point will need to be found. Turn left on another vague path heading upstream and follow this towards the

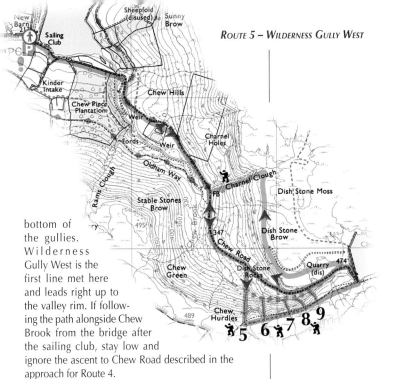

bottom of the gullies. Wilderness Gully West is the first line met here and leads right up to the valley rim. If following the path alongside Chew Brook from the bridge after the sailing club, stay low and ignore the ascent to Chew Road described in the approach for Route 4.

Route

Follow a line to suit conditions over the slabby rocks and boulders. In a really hard winter, ice can form over long sections of this route providing easy, but entertaining, ice climbing. Near the top, harder options are possible for those keen enough to have a go. From the top, follow the valley rim eastwards to **Chew Reservoir** and descend Chew Road back to the car park.

LINKS/EXTENSIONS

For more scrambling, from the reservoir follow the path along the edge of the moor, north of Chew Road, and go past Dish Stone Brow to descend Charnel Clough (Route 4, omitting the slabs at the top) and return to the car park along Chew Road.

ROUTE 6

Wilderness Gully East

Start/Finish	Car park at Dove Stones Reservoir, SE 013 036
Height gain	130m
Grade and rating	2/3 (summer and winter) ***

A long scramble with several distinct pitches, leading from Chew Brook all the way up to the plateau edge, this is a Pennine classic, providing great sport in any conditions. Best of all in a spell of fine weather when the water-washed rock is dry and really rather sensuous, or in a good winter, under snow and ice, when ice-climbing gear is essential and the use of a rope is recommended. After a period of hard frost, even without snow, it can provide a really entertaining scramble on thin ice.

Approach

As for Route 5, but continue a little further up the line of Chew Brook, over ground that can often be 'boggy', until the next obvious gully line is reached.

Route

Scramble over several short rock steps to begin with. The first of these can be awkward in very wet conditions and a short detour to the left may be needed to avoid a wetting. Steady clambering then leads to the first major rock obstacle. The usual line follows ledges in the corner on the left, with a step right near the top. Climb further short rock steps to reach a final steepening where you can either climb a shallow crack/groove line on the right (easy on

First ice pitch in Wilderness Gully East (Photograph: Chris Sleaford)

good holds) or on the left, in a corner, a short chimney with a tricky exit. Now follow the easiest line to the top.

LINKS/EXTENSIONS
As for Route 5.

ROUTE 7
Wilderness Gully Far East

Start/Finish	Car park at Dove Stones Reservoir, SE 013 036
Height gain	75m
Grade and rating	1/2 (summer and winter)

A shallow gully line formed by water action, with a tricky entry and some loose rock that will require careful handling. This is the next line up to the plateau and a little shorter than the previous two routes.

Approach
As for Route 6, but continue further up **Chew Brook** as best you can until you spot the line. A quite large scooped slab lying back into the slope near the bottom is a good marker.

Route
Climb up to and over the awkward slab, which can be passed on the left (some grass) or by the very steep grassy bank on the right. Above this another small pitch is followed by clambering over boulders and small rock steps to the valley rim.

LINKS/EXTENSIONS
As for Route 5.

Approaching the slab at the bottom of the gully

ROUTE 8
Wilderness Gully Far Far East

Start/Finish	Car park at Dove Stones Reservoir, SE 013 036
Height gain	60m
Grade and rating	1 (summer), 1/2 (winter)

This is the fourth line up to the plateau, but once again shorter than the previous routes: a very shallow gully line formed by water action, somewhat marred by grass and loose rock. Best when dry, but a soaking awaits any slip from the greasy pole! The approach as described is more exciting than anything on the route.

Greasy pole action for Tom in Chew Brook approaching foot of route

This can all be avoided by staying on the left-hand bank and ascending steep grassy ledges to the left of the waterfall.

Approach

As for Route 7, but continue up **Chew Brook** to a deep pool beneath a waterfall. In the past, someone has wedged a short length of telegraph pole against the side wall of the pool to the right of the waterfall. Shuffle feet across the pole with hands on the wall (interesting when greasy), then step left onto the waterfall. A high layaway hold can help to surmount this. When wet, the use of a knee, elbow, anything, will all help! ◄

Route

Immediately after the waterfall, look for a shallow rocky corner leaning back slightly left. There is some grass and loose rock. Climb the corner with care and scramble up the blocky shallow gully line to a less interesting section. Things improve as height is gained, leading to a finish through large blocks close to the edge of the plateau.

LINKS/EXTENSIONS

As for Route 5.

ROUTE 9
Wilderness Gully Far Far Far East

Start/Finish	Car park at Dove Stones Reservoir, SE 013 036
Height gain	45m
Grade and rating	1 (summer and winter)

This is the last of the three shallow gully lines included here and the shortest, being towards the top end of Chew Road. It can dry more quickly than the other gullies after rain.

Approach
As for Route 8, but continue up **Chew Brook** to a small waterfall that can be bypassed using a grassy corner on the right.

Route
Follow the obvious line of water-washed rock leading up the hillside just after the waterfall. Really only easy clambering on fairly sound rock leading once more to the valley rim.

LINKS/EXTENSIONS
As for Route 5. There is another, shorter route to be had on these slopes, just before the hillside and the line of the brook converge near **Chew Reservoir**. Clean rock leads over steep steps to the top.

ROUTE 10

Chew Brook

Start/Finish	Car park at Dove Stones Reservoir, SE 013 036
Height gain	150m
Grade and rating	1 (summer and winter)

Following Chew Brook in its entirety from the bridge at the bottom can be entertaining, with a number of short waterfalls to negotiate plus the greasy pole traverse mentioned in Route 8. Ice will form in a good winter, but this is dependent on the amount of water coming down the brook as too much will prevent it forming apart from near the banks. It makes for a more exciting outing (obviously) than simply walking up Chew Road to visit the reservoir.

Approach

As for Route 4, but at the bridge (SE 019 032) take the path on the right of the stream to the bottom of Route 5.

Route

Stay with the stream bed, passing below Routes 5–9, seeking as much interest as possible until halted by the dam wall! Return to the car park down Chew Road or descend Charnel Clough (Route 4) as described in the links for Route 5.

LINKS/EXTENSIONS

As for Routes 5–9, descending Charnel Clough.

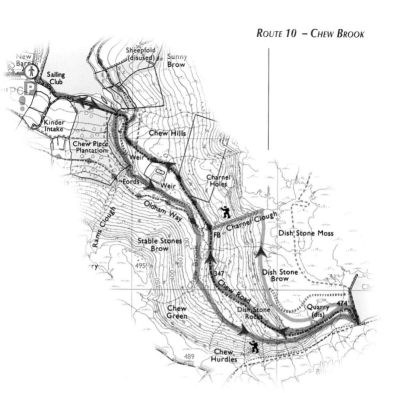

Greasy pole walked, waterfall ascended, a satisfied look back into Chew Brook

THE CROWDEN AREA

Gateway into the valley of Crowden Great Brook

This section covers the area to the north side of the A628 Woodhead Road where it passes through the Longdendale Valley. There is a youth hostel and campsite at Crowden with car parking and toilet facilities. The area as a whole is never really busy once away from the Pennine Way, which passes through Crowden before heading for the notorious peat bogs of Black Hill.

The historically important rock-climbing crag of Laddow Rocks sits above the valley of Crowden Great Brook, and there are several other notable rock outcrops around here too; Lad's Leap and the shorter buttresses of Bareholme Crag are among the better known. Generally speaking, these crags have lost their appeal to the modern rock climber, but in days gone by Laddow in particular was a very popular climbing venue where many aspiring rock tyros first cut their teeth. Laddow is also famous for its 'cave', and a spooky bivouac can be enjoyed here if you want to soak up some of the crag's history.

It was also at Laddow Rocks, in the aftermath of a climbing accident in November 1928, that the call for better facilities to aid victims of accidents in the mountains gained momentum, eventually leading to the Mountain Rescue Service as we know it today. A climber, Edgar Pryor, was knocked off Long Climb by a climber falling from above and suffered a fractured skull and a broken femur. A few months later the leg had to be amputated. The attending surgeon, Wilson Hey, was convinced that the carry down from the crag using a stretcher formed from fence posts or a signpost (accounts vary), and the resultant jarring, had contributed greatly to the trauma suffered by Pryor. Thus began a search for a better stretcher (eventually the 'Thomas Stretcher', named after its designer), and Hey went on to play a leading role in bringing about the setting up and equipping of designated Mountain Rescue Posts with improved rescue and medical supplies.

ROUTE 11
Oaken Clough

Start/Finish	Crowden car park, SK 073 993
Height gain	75m
Grade and rating	2/3 (summer), 2 (winter) **

An excellent scramble over a series of short pitches of water-washed rock, mixed with cascades and pools, finishing on the Pennine Way. Easy-angled clambering is encountered at first, getting steeper (and sometimes wetter) as height is gained, where excellent scrambling on clean, sound rock can be enjoyed. In winter, though unlikely to freeze fully, it can provide a very interesting ice/snow scramble.

Approach

From the car park reach and then follow the right bank of **Crowden Great Brook** heading north. There are several tracks and paths here, and it can get confusing, but once past the farm buildings things become clearer. Follow the road past the campsite and farm. Go through the gate on the right-hand fork in the road. Before the youth hostel take a track on the right to go up through a gate then walk horizontally by a wall to cross a stile at a footbridge (SK 070 999) over **Crowden Little Brook**. Cross the bridge and swing right, climbing gently up a path (not obvious) to another stile on the left. The path rises then falls towards another footbridge over Crowden Great Brook, past old concrete hut bases.

Do not cross this bridge; stay on the right bank of the brook and follow the path until opposite the entrance to Oakenclough Brook (SE 061 009). Trees show the line of the brook, which at this point is not obvious. Cross Crowden Great Brook and walk up into **Oaken Clough** using a narrow path well hidden by heather and bilberry bushes.

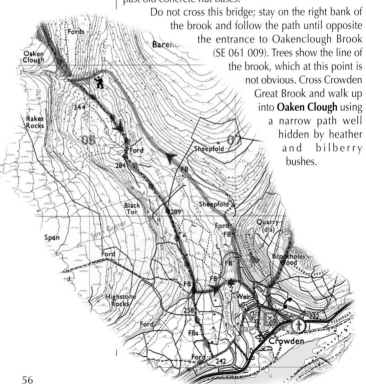

The long cascade in Oaken Clough

Route

Try to keep to the rock as much as possible in order to avoid any damage to the trees and other vegetation along the route. Scramble up easily to the first real obstacle, a cascade above a small pool. A steep crack in the right corner, using a good layaway hold, leads to a move right up slabby rock. This section can be avoided by using a steep grassy groove on the right. Above is a bigger cascade, which is usually climbed on the left-hand side to a pool, where a move to the right corner leads to a position below a huge chockstone.

Depending on conditions, either climb the corner or rocks on the left, or use a through-route under the chockstone to a ledge and step up right to get above the chockstone. The next small waterfall is climbed by a short groove and corner on the right. Walk up easily to the next fall, which is usually passed on the right by a corner flake with a hard pull over to a dirty ledge. Now simply follow the stream upwards over small rock steps to a meeting with the **Pennine Way**. For a short day, follow this south towards **Crowden** to find the descent path (SK 067 995) back towards the youth hostel and the car park.

LINKS/EXTENSIONS

Link A

Highly recommended! From the top of **Oaken Clough** follow the **Pennine Way** towards **Laddow Rocks**. After about 250m take a fork to the left (SE 056 013) onto the path to **Chew Reservoir**. Walk down Chew Road and climb **Wilderness Gully East** (Route 6). Of course, any of the other Wilderness Gullies could be ascended. From the top, walk back to **Chew Reservoir** and retrace the outward route back to the **Pennine Way**. Continue from here as described in the main route above. This link adds about 6km to the day.

Link B

As above, but from **Chew Reservoir** follow the path along the edge of the plateau past Dish Stone Brow to descend Charnel Clough (Route 4). Walk up the Chew Road back to Chew Reservoir or ascend one of the Wilderness Gullies (Routes 5–9). Return as for Link A above.

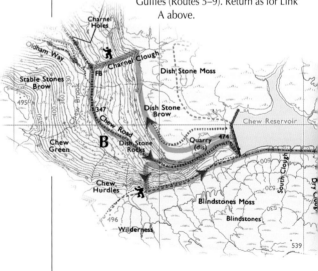

Above the chockstone pitch near the top of Oaken Clough

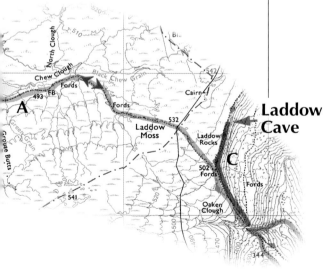

Link C

If all that is desired is a unique place for a coffee break, try visiting **Laddow Rocks** to see the cave, which is steeped in history and quite atmospheric. It can be found by following the **Pennine Way** past the crag and then dropping down the climbers' path at the northern end of the crag. A solo bivouac in here can be quite an experience!

If you have some rock-climbing experience and are happy to carry a rope and a few runners up the previous route, you can also do some more scrambling at this point on Laddow Rocks. Where the clough meets the **Pennine Way** join the lower traverse path that leads to the right towards **Laddow Rocks**. Follow the path horizontally until the rocks come into view. Aim for the fairly obvious square 'slabby' buttress near the left-hand end of the main crag. There is no clear upward path, so try to find the easiest line, up steep grass, heading for almost the lowest point of the crag. This is the climbers' route 'Staircase', an excellent climb, graded 'Moderate' in the climbers' guidebook but good value for this grade. Climb the steep and wonderfully exposed slab to a big stance and belay. A series of short corners lead easily to join the Pennine Way at the top. But be warned, there is no sound belay here and you may have to simply wedge yourself into the trench that is the Pennine Way at this point.

Return to the Pennine Way, retrace the route to the top of **Oaken Clough** and return to the car park as for the main route description.

EXTENSION

A longer option (c10km) is to continue along the **Pennine Way** to **Black Hill** and return over **Tooleyshaw Moss** to **Crowden** (see Option 1 of The Black Hill Round below); on a warm summer's day it is a really good trip.

ROUTE 12
Coombes Clough

Start/Finish	Crowden car park, SK 073 993
Height gain	100m
Grade and rating	1/2 (summer)

This is a long south-facing clough with a series of short pitches and pools leading to the edge of the moor at Lad's Leap; the best scrambling is in the upper half. Perched high above the A628 Woodhead Road, this route has a rather tedious approach, but this is rewarded by some wonderful positions and views across Torside Reservoir to the south.

Approach

From the car park walk up the road towards the youth hostel. At the fork by the farm, go left through a gate and carry on to join the **Pennine Way**. Head west briefly to pick up an indistinct path heading towards a group of barns (Highstones, SK 061 990). Find a way over the walls here to gain open country and contour round on vague sheep tracks, through dense bracken, to emerge just above the trees at the foot of Coombes Clough proper (SK 054 993). ▶

Cautionary note: the banks here are high and undercut, so stay clear of the edge until it is possible to contour into the streambed.

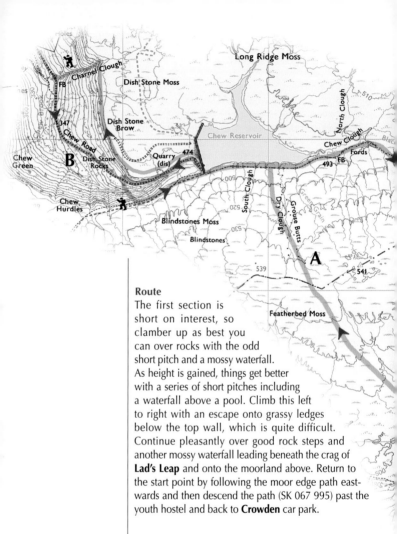

Route

The first section is
short on interest, so
clamber up as best you
can over rocks with the odd
short pitch and a mossy waterfall.
As height is gained, things get better
with a series of short pitches including
a waterfall above a pool. Climb this left
to right with an escape onto grassy ledges
below the top wall, which is quite difficult.
Continue pleasantly over good rock steps and
another mossy waterfall leading beneath the crag of
Lad's Leap and onto the moorland above. Return to
the start point by following the moor edge path eastwards and then descend the path (SK 067 995) past the
youth hostel and back to **Crowden** car park.

LINKS/EXTENSIONS

Link A/B

For a longer day (8–9km), walk northwestwards from **Lad's Leap** across the moor along Hollins Clough and over **Featherbed Moss** to **Chew Reservoir** to complete one of the suggestions (Links A or B) for Route 11, returning via **Laddow Rocks** and the **Pennine Way**.

The Black Hill Round

Not listed here as a numbered scramble, this traditional and popular outing from Crowden can be given a bit of a twist to offer a new slant on an old favourite. In both options scrambling content is minimal, but interest levels remain high for most of the way.

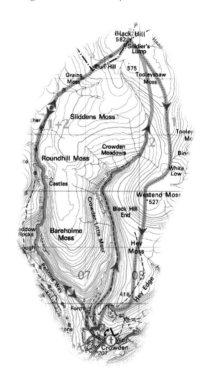

Map on this page at 1:50,000

Option 1 (clockwise, 13–14km) Follow **Crowden Great Brook** northwards (using the streambed for interest in the later stages) going past the **Castles** (SE 063 022) to join the **Pennine Way**. Note that if the brook is in spate some serious route decisions may be called for, as crossing and re-crossing the brook will be tricky. It may be necessary to stay high on the right bank until one of the fords to the north of the Castles can be used. Follow the Pennine Way to the summit of **Black Hill** (SE 078 047). Return south over **Tooleyshaw Moss** and Westend Moss, following the path back to **Crowden**.

Option 2 (anti-clockwise, c12km) Walk up the track parallel to **Crowden Little Brook** until the banks begin to close in and steepen and then drop down to the brook itself, which here flows through a mini gorge leading to a delightful waterfall on the right (SE 074 022). It is usually possible to scramble up this on the left. Now follow the brook until forced back out onto the moor and continue northwards to the summit of **Black Hill**. Return along the **Pennine Way** until near the head of **Crowden Great Brook** proper (SE 061 025) and follow this back to **Crowden** rather than staying on the Pennine Way.

BLEAKLOW

This section covers the whole of the area south of Longdendale and to the north of the A57 Snake Pass road. It is generally not as busy as Kinder Scout, which lies further south, and is viewed by many as uninteresting. In fact, it seems as though Bleaklow has had a bad press ever since pen was first put to paper and, not surprisingly, that old grump Wainwright was very dismissive of its charms. Its reputation as a dark and unforgiving place, not to be lingered in, may arise from the fact that many people's sole experience of the area is based on a crossing of the plateau as part of an attempt on the Pennine Way, which means that they have had to 'push on' whatever the weather and conditions underfoot. The paths through the peat can resemble a sticky morass, especially after heavy rain or in the winter months when not frozen, and it is quite possible for the unwary to sink up to their knees when crossing an open stretch of bog. In poor visibility one peat hag looks much like any other, and without careful compass work it is easy to get lost.

In recent years, however, the Pennine Way path has undergone a lot of improvement work and the vast tracts of bare peat have been reseeded as part of the Moors for the Future project, so things are not so 'bleak' as they once were and the new grasses are helping to stabilise the peat. While it remains true that, once on the plateau, prominent landmarks are few and far between, around the flanks there are many wonderful places worthy of a day's outing. Shining Clough, Wildboar Clough and Torside Clough present a rugged edge in the north, whereas Yellowslacks Brook in the west and the cloughs rising from the Doctor's Gate path in the southwest are somewhat gentler. Meanwhile, the valley of the River Alport to the south and the Upper Derwent Valley in the east present a variety of landscapes along their lengths that are simply stunning to walk through. Dotted amongst all this are delightful, quite remote spots such as The Grinah Stones, Grains in the Water and The Rocking Stones, all of which can often be enjoyed in solitary peace and quiet.

So, to see Bleaklow in a new light perhaps, try the routes listed here, most of which make use of the features mentioned above to reach the plateau. Wildboar Clough is the best known and provides a classic scramble in both summer and winter. However, other surprises await!

Wildboar Clough: the large waterfall pitch in winter (Route 17)

67

LONGDENDALE/
BLEAKLOW NORTH

ROUTE 13
Shining Clough

Start/Finish	Car park on B6105 at Woodhead Reservoir, SK 082 993 or car park at Torside Reservoir, SK 068 983
Height gain	100m
Grade and rating	2 (summer), 2/3 (winter) **

This is an excellent route with several sections of good scrambling: an undercut entry pitch is usually impassable (in winter, snow and ice can 'bank up' here to enable an ascent to be made). Above this, two steep pitches, separated by easy scrambling, are followed by several shorter ones leading to the moor above. Some parts seem permanently greasy, perhaps due to the enclosed nature of the clough, but there is some really nice water-washed rock to scramble on too. During a hard, cold winter the stream can freeze quickly due its north-facing aspect and this often results in a long continuous ribbon of ice forming, visible high on the hillside above the Woodhead Reservoir from the A628 below. It presents what may be one of this area's best-kept secrets in the form of a big ice pitch up the first steep section of the clough. This is more the terrain of experienced ice climbers, but with the right gear it could be top-roped to enable lesser mortals to have a go. Above this, the rest of the route provides a lengthy 'ice scramble'.

Approach

Park in the small car park at the southwest corner of **Woodhead Reservoir** on the B6105, adjacent to the Longdendale Trail. If the plan is to link Shining Clough with an ascent of Wildboar Clough and a return down Torside Clough (see Link B) then the best start point is the pay-and-display car park on the south side of the B6105 at **Torside Reservoir**. From there, reach the Woodhead Reservoir car park by walking about 2km eastwards along the Longdendale Trail.

Just above the Woodhead Reservoir car park there is a tarmacked track. Walk left (eastwards) along the track for about 1.5km to the 'open country' signpost (SK 094 994) just short of **The Lodge**. A path leads uphill from here. Follow the path, keeping to the right of a fence and crossing a stile of sorts where this fence meets another, before curving round to the left and across another stile to reach the streambed of **Shining Clough**. The path now leads upwards through trees at the side of the stream and leads into the clough proper a little further on.

Easy scrambling above the entry pitch can be reached by descending from the broad ledge at the end of the traverse path (Photograph: Chris Sleaford)

Route

Continue up the line of the clough past several cascades. Take care climbing over what can be green and slippery rock (or avoid most of this by taking to the grassier left bank) to arrive below the entry pitch, which is deeply undercut at its base and often wet. It is worth having a close look but, if or when deterred, retreat down the clough a little to where the eastern slopes are less steep and then work up grass and heather around a rock outcrop to find a vague traverse path that leads back into the clough to a broad flat ledge.

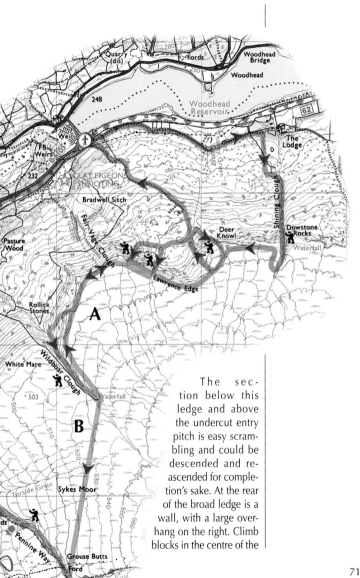

The section below this ledge and above the undercut entry pitch is easy scrambling and could be descended and re-ascended for completion's sake. At the rear of the broad ledge is a wall, with a large overhang on the right. Climb blocks in the centre of the

Final moves onto the top of the second large wall

wall (often wet) to gain the big ledge on the left (the use of a knee may help) and then move left to finish up the corner. Now move over a fairly level section to a second, higher wall. This will be greasy if wet, but can be climbed on the left using blocks and cracks with good holds. There follows a series of easy short walls and rock steps that lead with continued interest to the top of the clough.

The easiest return to the start point is to find the path that runs along the edge of the moor and follow this west to descend the hillside (around SK 090 985) to the west of **Deer Knowl**. Descend further to join the old quarry track (SK 089 988) that leads down to the tarmacked track just above the **Woodhead Reservoir** car park.

LINKS/EXTENSIONS

If a bog trot to Bleaklow Head is not part of the plan, the scrambling can be extended by one of the following options.

Extension

Having descended to the west of **Deer Knowl**, try one or more of the routes in this area (Routes 14–16) before returning to the car park as described above.

Link A

For a longer day out, add an ascent of Wildboar Clough (Route 17). Reach this by walking along the edge path past **Deer Knowl** and **Lawrence Edge** to the west. Look for a steep descent in the area of the **Rollick Stones** (around SK 081 983) before reaching **Wildboar Clough**. 'Rollick' carefully down the slope until you can contour round into the start of Wildboar Clough itself. Return to the **Woodhead Reservoir** car park by walking back eastwards along the edge to descend west of Deer Knowl as described in the main route description.

Link B

To descend Torside Clough (Route 18) from the top of **Wildboar Clough**, head almost due south towards John Track Well at the bottom of Wild Boar Grain (SK 081

964). Join the streambed of **Torside Clough** and follow this all the way to the bottom. Join the **Pennine Way** back to the Longdendale Trail to return to either of the car parks.

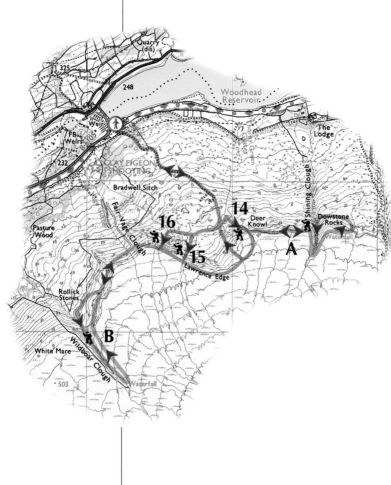

ROUTE 14
Deer Knowl

Start/Finish	Car park on B6105 at Woodhead Reservoir, SK 082 993
Height gain	40m
Grade and rating	2/3 (summer), 2 (winter) *

This crag (SK 092 987) sits on the northern edge of the Bleaklow plateau above the Woodhead Reservoir and, when combined with the routes on Lawrence Edge, there is enough interest here to justify a visit for a short afternoon's entertainment. The route follows the obvious light-coloured line towards the western end of the crag. It may look improbable from below, but it is a surprisingly good route with excellent scrambling over clean, mostly sound rock leading to the path along the edge of the plateau. A shame it's not longer!

Moving up to the right on the first wall (Photograph: Chris Sleaford)

Photograph: Chris Sleaford

Approach

Park in the small car park at the southwest corner of **Woodhead Reservoir** on the B6105, adjacent to the Longdendale Trail. Walk up to the tarmacked track above the car park, turn left and, at the side of the first pylon, join the obvious track that leads uphill to the old quarry workings. At the top of the track ignore the curve around to the right into the quarry and instead continue uphill, following a vague path through grass and heather to the bottom of the final slopes to the right of **Deer Knowl**, then choose a line and traverse over to the left to reach the bottom of the route.

Route

Move easily over blocks and up a narrower section to a small bay backed by a steep wall with a narrow ledge at about one-third height. Step onto the ledge and, working from left to right, move over to, and up, the corner on the right. Easier ground leads to another steep section, where a step up gives access to a 'hidden' groove on the right. This provides excellent scrambling on steep clean rock to the top. Return to the car by reversing the approach on the old quarry track.

Photograph: Chris Sleaford

LINKS/EXTENSIONS

Link A

Head east on the path for an ascent of **Shining Clough** (Route 13). The slopes bounding the western side of the clough are very steep and prevent a safe, direct descent into it, so continue along the path and around the top of the clough towards the climbers' crag of Shining Clough Rocks. Descend the hillside (around SK 097 987) before reaching the western end of the crag to find the vague traverse path that contours round from here into **Shining Clough**, finishing at the broad flat ledge above the entry pitch. The slopes here are still steep, so take care.

Link B

Head west on the path for an ascent of **Wildboar Clough** (see Route 13, Link A, for details of the best approach).

Extension

Descend the slope to the west of **Deer Knowl** and head into the hollow below **Lawrence Edge** to ascend Route 15 or 16.

ROUTE 15

Lawrence Edge No 1

Start/Finish	Car park on B6105 at Woodhead Reservoir, SK 082 993
Height gain	50m
Grade and rating	1 (summer and winter)

Lawrence Edge (SK 087 985) is just to the west of Deer Knowl and at first glance there appears to be scope for more routes than the ones described here. However, these seem to offer most in terms of a continuous line. Some loose rock is encountered at first, but there are several good clean rock steps higher up.

Approach

As for Route 14, but after leaving the quarry track and walking uphill a little, work over to the right until the flat area below **Lawrence Edge** and behind the quarry workings comes into view.

On the very left (eastern) end of the crag is a gully line rising up the hillside at a shallow angle. Further right there are two steeper gully lines close together. This route is the left hand of the latter two and not the most promising at first sight, but the one to the right is less continuous. Follow a vague path through the grass and heather (some hidden rocks underfoot) to the bottom of the gully.

Route

Where the gully steepens, clamber over blocks and water-washed rock steps eventually arriving at a steep, undercut wall. This can be avoided by taking to steep grass on the right or by circling around and upwards on the slope to the left. Straightforward and enjoyable scrambling on clean rock leads from here to the top.

LINKS/EXTENSIONS
As for Route 14 to **Shining Clough** or **Wildboar Clough**, or descend the hillside to the east of **Lawrence Edge** and contour round for an ascent of **Deer Knowl** (Route 14).

ROUTE 16
Lawrence Edge No 2

Start/Finish	Car park on B6105 at Woodhead Reservoir, SK 082 993
Height gain	50m
Grade and rating	1 (summer and winter)

A contrast to Route 15, this is more open with fewer rock steps and more boulders to overcome.

Large boulders are encountered at first with some loose rock halfway up. It could be used as a descent, but care needed if wet.

Approach
As for Route 15, but go further over and slightly downhill towards the right-hand end of the crag where there is a sandy level area. The line of the gully is obvious from below, slanting up to the right as it heads for the steeper rocks at the top.

Route
Clamber over large blocks and boulders to begin with, working upwards to a narrowing of the gully that leads towards a rock tower near the top. Go up this narrow section on small blocks or, over to the right, a short rock 'staircase'. Finish up the easy-angled ramp to the right of the tower to finish on the plateau.

LINKS/EXTENSIONS
As for Route 15.

ROUTE 17
Wildboar Clough

Start/Finish	Car park on B6105 at Torside Reservoir, SK 068 983
Height gain	120m
Grade and rating	2/3 (summer and winter) ***

This is the Bleaklow classic, good in any conditions: an excellent and quite long scramble following the streambed and taking in a series of waterfalls and small rocky steps. It faces north, so after a reasonable period of frost the stream freezes, providing good sport at a reasonable standard with several short ice pitches. It has become very popular with people practising their ice climbing and can be quite busy on winter weekends (less busy at other times of the year).

Approach
Park at the **Torside Reservoir** pay-and-display car park, signposted to the side of the B6105. Walk up to the Longdendale Trail and turn left, heading eastwards, for about 200m. Look out for a small signpost pointing to Wildboar Clough on the right. Steps lead over a stile onto a concessionary path, which avoids the clay-pigeon shooting area further on (avoid this at all costs!). Follow the path up through woodland to reach a fence and open moorland. Follow the narrow path on the right bank of **Wildboar Clough** until it is possible to get into the streambed. ◀ You can also get into the streambed at the first opportunity and clamber all the way along it, over boulders, until below the first pitch.

It is also possible to cross the stream lower down, near the stile, and use a vague path on the left bank until you feel like getting involved.

Moving up to the large waterfall pitch

Route

The first obstacle is usually climbed on the left using an awkward wide crack to the left of a slabby rock. Follow the streambed easily to below the next little pitch,

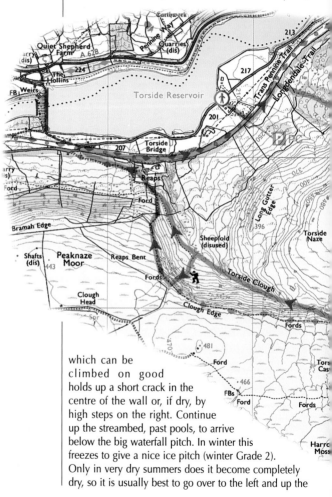

which can be climbed on good holds up a short crack in the centre of the wall or, if dry, by high steps on the right. Continue up the streambed, past pools, to arrive below the big waterfall pitch. In winter this freezes to give a nice ice pitch (winter Grade 2). Only in very dry summers does it become completely dry, so it is usually best to go over to the left and up the corner on good holds. Step carefully left, then up and back right to get above it. More small pitches lead easily to another steep little wall, which can be climbed by a crack in the left corner. Move up until a long reach over the top reveals a hidden hold and use this to roll over onto the sloping slab. The clough continues with some interest until it eventually levels out to merge with the moorland above.

If not visiting Bleaklow Head, head southwards for about 1.25km, towards the junction of Wildboar Grain and **Torside Clough** (SK 081 965).

▶ Descend Torside by following the streambed all the way down, rejoining the **Pennine Way** further down

On the way down there is an option to include an ascent of Torside Gully (Route 19)

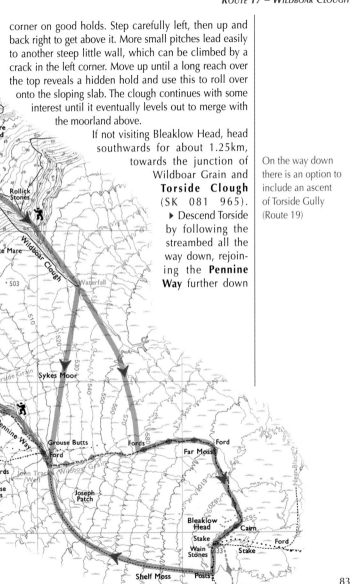

The central crack of the second pitch

the valley and returning along the Longdendale Trail to the start point.

LINKS/EXTENSIONS

Extension

To visit Bleaklow Head, walk roughly southeast from the top of Wildboar Clough over open moorland for about 1km to meet the Pennine Way where it runs adjacent to Wildboar Grain. Follow the path eastwards and then south to **Bleaklow Head**. From here, ignore the Pennine Way and pick up a path that heads due south towards the Hern Stones. After about 200m another path (SK 092 958) leads off to the west. Follow this as it swings northwest to the junction of Wildboar Grain and **Torside Clough** (SK 081 965) and rejoin the main route.

ROUTE 18
Torside Clough

Start/Finish	Car park on B6105 at Torside Reservoir, SK 068 983
Height gain	150m
Grade and rating	1 (summer and winter) *

Interesting and easy scrambling, either in ascent or descent, in a clough that has it all – nice cascades, waterfalls and pools of varying depths – but some loose rock. The amount of scrambling involved depends on how soon the streambed is entered, although as the clough narrows in the upper reaches there is no other option. It provides an entertaining and not too arduous alternative approach to Bleaklow Head compared with the usual Pennine Way options.

Approach
Park as for Route 17. Walk westwards along the Longdendale Trail for about 1.2km to pick up the **Pennine Way** where it meets the trail (SK 058 980). Follow the Pennine Way back eastwards to arrive above **Reaps Farm**. Where the path forks (SK 063 977), take the smaller path to the left. This leads into **Torside Clough** where, after passing through a gate, Torside Rocks (SK 064 972) come into view on the hillside to the right. Continue along the track to the concrete water collector.

Route
A vague path follows the right bank (when looking up the clough). Follow this and the water's edge past a nice cascade. Just above here, cross over to the left bank (can be tricky) and follow this all the way into a more shattered

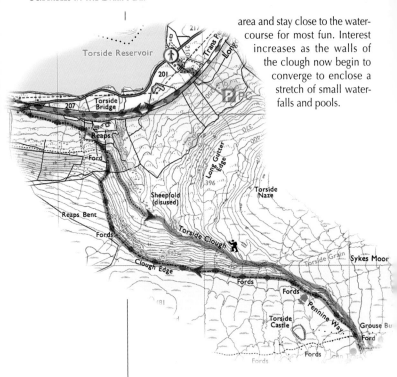

area and stay close to the water-course for most fun. Interest increases as the walls of the clough now begin to converge to enclose a stretch of small water-falls and pools.

Just at the exit of this narrow section there is a steep, clean, blocky corner on the right bank (often wet) that leads into a shallow gully climbing all the way up to the Pennine Way above. This gully can be ascended with interest (at Grade 2) and at the top there is a small cairn, presumably to show the entry point for what would be a difficult descent into Torside Clough. If not seduced by the gully, continue up the clough, which retains interest as far as the junction with Wildboar Grain. Here (SK 081 965) Torside Clough is crossed by the Pennine Way, which provides a straightforward return to the northwest following the valley rim back to the Longdendale Trail and the car park.

The optional gully that rises from Torside Clough to meet the Pennine Way on the moorland above

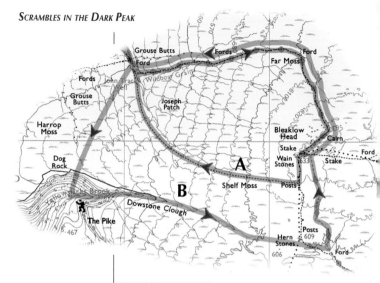

LINKS/EXTENSIONS

Link A

From the junction with Wildboar Grain the easiest route to Bleaklow Head is to follow the **Pennine Way** eastward along Wildboar Grain and then south to **Bleaklow Head**. Return to the junction via the lesser path (SK 092 958) mentioned in the extension for Route 17, and then continue along the valley rim as described above to return to the car park.

Link B

For a more interesting (but longer) route to Bleaklow Head from the junction, cross the moor in a southwesterly direction, aiming for a point just east of **Dog Rock** (SK 076 958) above **Yellowslacks Brook**. Descend diagonally into the brook to where the valley sides close in below the impressive waterfall. Ascend the brook (see Route 20) and continue eastwards to the **Hern Stones** (SK 092 954) and then north to **Bleaklow Head**. Return to the car park by following the **Pennine Way** to the north and then west down Wildboar Grain to return to the junction. Continue along the valley rim as described above to return to the car park.

ROUTE 19
Torside Gully

Start/Finish	Car park on B6105 at Torside Reservoir, SK 068 983
Height gain	70m
Grade and rating	2 (summer and winter) **

This route offers engaging scrambling up a series of short steep steps in a gully-type environment with interesting positions. It is a surprisingly good line, not at all obvious, providing an excellent alternative way of getting from the Longdendale Trail to the Bleaklow plateau via Clough Edge and has finishing holds on the Pennine Way itself! It only carries a lot of water after very heavy rain, when it would be briefly impossible to complete the route. In snowy conditions it can provide an entertaining route that may need winter equipment, but it holds very little ice.

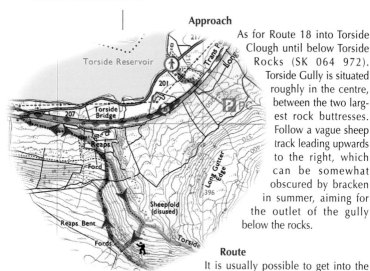

Approach

As for Route 18 into Torside Clough until below Torside Rocks (SK 064 972). Torside Gully is situated roughly in the centre, between the two largest rock buttresses. Follow a vague sheep track leading upwards to the right, which can be somewhat obscured by bracken in summer, aiming for the outlet of the gully below the rocks.

Route

It is usually possible to get into the streambed quite low down, as it is nearly always dry. Then go up a couple of small rock steps to reach the first real obstacle. This short steep pitch has good holds and leads to easier scrambling up short steps between grassy banks towards the obvious steepening of the gully. Here there are two more short steep steps that are climbed from good ledges. Now move up on rock, with grass incursions, to where a vague path leads right onto the crest of a ridge.

Follow this path and ascend two short rock steps in a nice position to a big ledge under steeper rock (a great place to take a refreshment break!). Traverse left on another vague grassy path to return to the main gully line and climb over several short rock steps to arrive below a final steepening. This steep section can be avoided by moving up grass on the right, otherwise a technical foot change allows a good ledge to be reached. Ascend more rock to final moves onto the **Pennine Way**, which can be followed back to the Longdendale Trail to return to the car park.

LINKS/EXTENSIONS

Link A
From the top of Torside Gully, follow the **Pennine Way** eastwards until it meets the stream in **Torside Clough** near the junction with Wildboar Grain (SK 081 965). From here, descend Torside Clough (Route 18) to rejoin the outward path below Torside Gully and return to the car park along the Longdendale Trail.

Link B
A longer option would be to follow the directions in Link B for Route 18, which heads from the junction to **Yellowslacks Brook** before going on to **Bleaklow Head**. Once back at the junction, either follow the **Pennine Way** along the valley rim or descend **Torside Clough** (Route 18) to return to the car park as above.

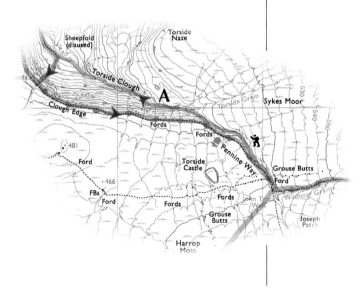

A large rock step about halfway up Torside Gully

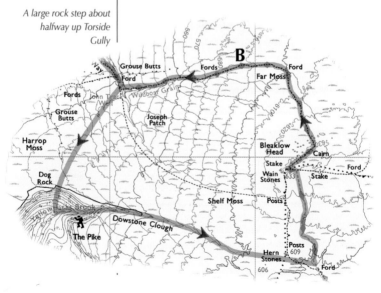

ROUTE 20
Yellowslacks Brook/Dowstone Clough

Start/Finish	On A57 Sheffield road east of Glossop, SK 056 942 or Shepley Street, Old Glossop, SK 046 948
Height gain	125m along whole route
Grade and rating	1 (summer and winter)

This route follows a well-defined, deep streambed with a nice waterfall and several short rock steps, best used as a link (where suggested) from one of the other routes as an interesting way to reach Bleaklow Head or Higher Shelf Stones. In a good winter, snow can linger a long time in the upper section of Dowstone Clough and form nevé. The route offers interesting scrambling with some pleasant sections on the gritstone bedrock. The initial waterfall is a good one and worth a visit even if it is not possible to ascend it direct. It would provide a very good ice pitch were it to freeze.

Approach

With most interest being towards the upper section of Dowstone Clough it is suggested that this route be included as a link from one of the others (Routes 18 and 21, for example). However, if a direct approach is desired try to park, without causing an obstruction, on the approach to the first sharp bend on the A57 Sheffield Road as it leaves Glossop. There will be a minimum walk of about 750m up to the bend in the road and the start of the track past **Mossy Lea Farm**. Follow the track to its junction with the **Doctor's Gate** path (SK 061 947) and turn right (east) onto this. Continue easily uphill, following the line of a wall, and through a gate into open country. Where the Doctor's Gate path drops off to the right, continue straight ahead. At the end of the wall continue uphill to pass a derelict shooting cabin from where to find a way into **Yellowslacks Brook**.

Alternatively, a shorter approach, which requires a steepish descent into the clough, involves parking in **Old Glossop** on, or as close as possible to, Shepley Street.

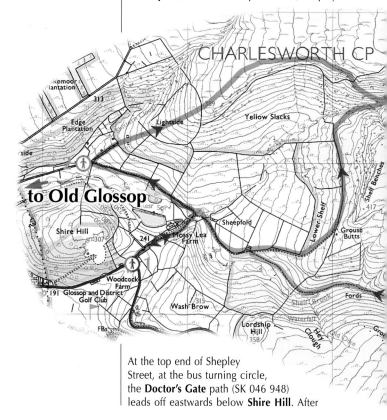

At the top end of Shepley Street, at the bus turning circle, the **Doctor's Gate** path (SK 046 948) leads off eastwards below **Shire Hill**. After about 1km a stile gives access to the spur of moorland (Lightside) rising to the northeast. Cross the stile, go uphill, and follow the well-worn track along the brow of **Yellow Slacks**, which gives great views back over Glossop. When roughly opposite the bottom of Wigan Clough (SK 073 954), carefully descend the steep slope into the bottom of **Yellowslacks Brook**.

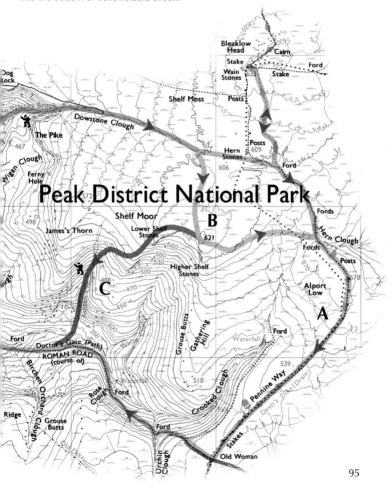

Route

Follow the line of the brook until the impressive waterfall that marks the start of the more interesting sections is reached. Once it has been decided that a direct assault on the waterfall might be a bit stiff, a clamber up the loose gully on the right leads to a grassy traverse line that can be followed back left into the clough above the waterfall (the traverse line may be difficult to spot, but there is a vague path). This leads to an impressive hollow and another waterfall. Drop down and cross the brook in order to scramble out using ledges on the left side of this second waterfall. Stay as close to the water as possible for most interest.

Once above the waterfalls, the gritstone bedrock leading into upper **Dowstone Clough** is very pleasant to walk on when dry. Some small rock steps add interest until eventually the clough merges with the plateau. Once again, several options now present themselves.

The first waterfall with the escape gully on the right

LINKS/EXTENSIONS

Link A

From the top of **Dowstone Clough**, follow a path on the left bank (often boggy) to head eastwards to the **Hern Stones** (SK 092 954) and then north to **Bleaklow Head** (SK 092 959). From here, follow the **Pennine Way** back southwards towards the Snake Pass (A57) to reach the junction with the **Doctor's Gate** path (SK 089 933), and follow this westwards back to **Glossop**.

Link B

Alternatively (if not visiting Bleaklow Head), where the path to the **Hern Stones** passes through an indistinct grassy area there is a tenuous path that leads off to the right and eventually drops into a sandy grough leading to the trig point at **Higher Shelf Stones** (SK 088 947), where you can read 100-year-old graffiti carved into the rocks. ▶ The **Pennine Way** can be joined by heading east or southeast across open moorland (1–1.5km) for a return to the car as in Link A.

Link C

From **Higher Shelf Stones** head west towards Lower Shelf Stones (SK 086 948) and make a descent of Ashton Clough (Route 21) to join the **Doctor's Gate** path lower down the valley and return to the car as in Link A above. However, Ashton Clough is more rewarding as an ascent.

The upgraded Pennine Way wends its way through the reseeded area of Bleaklow near the Hern Stones

This is a great viewpoint, much better than Bleaklow Head, although that does give a good view of the radio mast on Holme Moss! On a clear day there are extensive views all around.

ROUTE 21
Ashton Clough

Start/Finish	Snake Pass, SK 088 929 or Doctor's Gate path on A57, SK 096 929
Height gain	150m
Grade and rating	1 (summer and winter)

An easy scramble with several small waterfalls in the lower section and a number of short rock steps above. The lower waterfalls are often green and greasy but can be avoided to the right or left. The left-hand fork at the top of the clough contains some loose rock, which requires careful handling, but it is not as bad as it looks and there is some better scrambling at the very top.

The scrambling may be easy, but this route onto the tops is very satisfying. It is much better than the normal Pennine Way path and, when combined with one of the suggested links, makes for a good day out. Added interest is provided by the pieces of aircraft debris found nearly all the way up the clough. These are the remains of a Douglas C47 Dakota that crashed near James's Thorn in July 1945, killing all on board. Solo scramblers might like to reflect on this as they go past the wreckage. In winter, after heavy snowfall, deep névé can form on the slopes above the top end of the clough.

Approach

Park at the top of the **Snake Pass** (A57) where the Pennine Way crosses the road. Follow the **Pennine Way** north-wards to where it meets the **Doctor's Gate** path (SK 089 933) and turn left (west) onto the latter. Alternatively, as the A57 descends eastwards towards Sheffield, the first

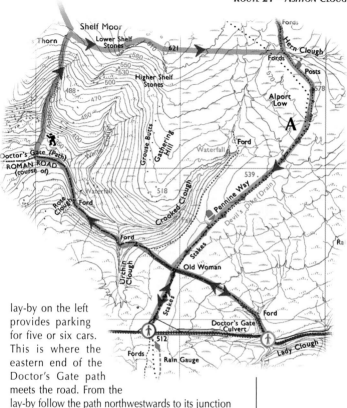

lay-by on the left provides parking for five or six cars. This is where the eastern end of the Doctor's Gate path meets the road. From the lay-by follow the path northwestwards to its junction with the **Pennine Way**.

From the **Pennine Way/Doctor's Gate** junction, follow the Doctor's Gate path northwestwards and downhill as it follows the line of **Shelf Brook**. There are great views of Lower and Higher Shelf Stones to the north and of the Bleaklow plateau and Crooked Clough to the east. The path begins to level off as it nears the bottom of White Clough (SK 082 941). Stay on the path until opposite the bottom of Ashton Clough (SK 080 941) where a descent to Shelf Brook can be made. Cross the brook and follow a faint path that leads from the right into Ashton Clough.

The fork at the top of the clough. The left-hand option gets better at the top

Route

Go past the first small waterfall (some may like to attempt to ascend this but, unless a wetting is desired, keep to the left) and also the second if there is too much water. After this go over several rock steps, gradually rising with interest past bits of undercarriage, engine and a large piece of fuselage. More rock steps eventually lead up to a fork in the clough. Don't be put off by appearances: the left fork is not as bad as it looks but does need care. Scramble over boulders and short steps to the final little pitch and some good rock towards the top. The right-hand fork is scrappier with smaller rock steps to overcome before reaching the top. From the top of the clough follow one of the links below.

LINKS/EXTENSIONS

Link A

If not visiting Bleaklow Head, go right and over the fence at a stile, to visit Lower Shelf Stones (SK 086 948) and on to the trig point at **Higher Shelf Stones** (SK 088 947) from where to enjoy great views. From the trig point head east or southeast across open moorland (1–1.5km) to join the **Pennine Way** and follow the path southwards back to the **Snake Pass** (A57).

Link B

To prolong the outing (by 4km, or about 5km if taking in **Bleaklow Head**), from the top of the clough go left to a stile over the fence and walk up the grassy knoll of **James's Thorn** towards spot height 572 (SK 08 1950).

▸ Now either go roughly northwest, aiming for the gap (SK 079 953) between **Ferny Hole** and **The Pike** and descend Wigan Clough (50m, easy, some loose rock) to its meeting (SK 073 954) with **Yellowslacks Brook**, or head off west of north, gradually descending towards a fence. Stay on the right side of this until a steep descent towards Yellowslacks Brook. Follow the water-washed streambed to the northeast, eventually arriving below the large waterfall as described in Route 20. Continue as for Route 20 (opting to visit **Bleaklow Head** or not) and eventually use the **Pennine Way** to return southwards to the start point.

On the way you should find the memorial stone for the crews of the C47 Dakota and a Lancaster bomber that crashed here in May 1945. Treat this area with respect; do not disturb any of the wreckage or memorials placed amongst it.

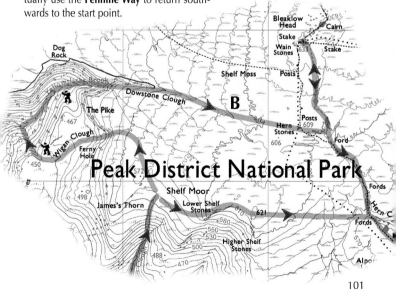

ROUTE 22

Alport Castles Tower

Start/Finish	Alport Bridge on A57, SK 142 896, Birchen Clough Bridge on A57, SK 109 913, Fairholmes Visitor Centre, SK 173 894 or lay-by on Fairholmes Road, SK 181 885
Height gain	20m from the 'col'
Grade and rating	1 (summer and winter)

The whole of the Alport Valley is a beautiful place to walk through and contains a variety of landscapes. The area known as Alport Castles (SK 142 915) is the result of a major landslip in the dim and distant past, and this route is a relatively short but steep scramble over the prominent tower (SK 141 914) that has been left standing amidst the wreckage: an easy approach across a grassy ridge before a steep ascent and descent of the final tower. Some of the rock is a little shattered so will need handling with respect. The route is well worth doing for the impressive surroundings and in winter, after a good period of frost and snowfall, it can be linked with Alport Castles Gully (Route 23) to provide good value for an easy Peak District winter outing.

Please note that restrictions due to bird nesting may be in place, so check with the BMC for up-to-date information when planning a visit.

Approach

There are a few options for a starting point:

1) There is very limited parking at Alport Bridge on the south side of the A57, but this does give the most direct approach as the entrance to **Alport Dale** is just across the road. Beware though, careless parking can

result in cars being 'blocked in' and a long wait for others to return from their outings.

2) An interesting alternative is to park higher up the Snake Pass (A57) at **Birchen Clough Bridge** and follow the route of the old Roman Road down to the entrance of **Alport Dale** (SK 140 897).

3) Another approach is from the **Fairholmes Visitor Centre** pay-and-display car park situated on the northern arm of **Ladybower Reservoir**. Follow a path from the side of the access road up and through the woods (signposted Lockerbrook) leading to **Lockerbrook Farm** (SK 165 894). The path heads south here for about 300m before turning back north uphill and then west to pass Bellhag Tor (SK 160 895) and Pasture Tor over **Rowlee Pasture** towards **Alport Castles**. Take the descent path (SK 145 912) to the south of Little Moor and, where the ground begins to level off, move across the slopes to the north to find the grassy ridge that leads over to **The Tower**.

4) Bellhag Tor can also be approached by a longer path starting near the lay-by on the Fairholmes Road.

Approaching from Option 1 or 2, follow the track up **Alport Dale** to **Alport Castles Farm** (SK 135 911). Take the circuitous path that leads eastwards to cross the footbridge over the River Alport before climbing the slope towards **Alport Castles**. Well before the top, go left over a fence and head north below Little Moor towards **The Tower**.

Route

The bottom of **The Tower** is reached by following a grassy ridge past a tree to a small 'col'. Now climb up rock and shale to an obvious ledge below a steepening in the rock. This can be taken direct up a small corner at Grade 2/3 (quite serious) or, for meeker souls, traverse left on the ledge around the corner to find a line to the top that keeps to the rock as far as possible. ▶ Follow the crest as closely as possible until near the western end. Descend to the left (west) down a slabby rock, then trend rightwards to the bottom. Alternatively, there is a corner chimney that could be descended. Now walk roughly northwest to the end of the big shale/rock cliff (Alport Castles Gully,

There is a good photo opportunity here, so stand on your head if you must!

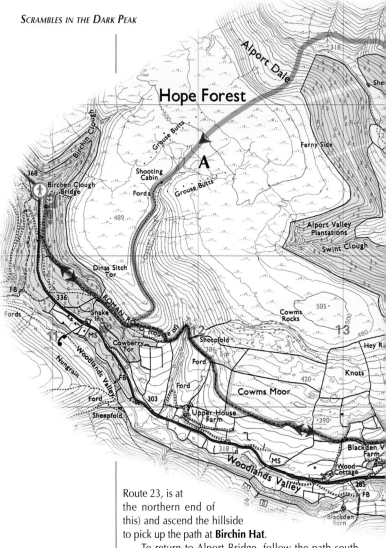

Route 23, is at
the northern end of
this) and ascend the hillside
to pick up the path at **Birchin Hat**.

To return to Alport Bridge, follow the path southeastwards and take the right-hand fork (SK 145 912) to
descend to **Alport Castles Farm** and the outward path

back to the A57. Similarly, take this route to rejoin the Roman Road at the entrance to **Alport Dale** to return to Birchen Clough Bridge.

to Fairholmes Visitor Centre and Fairholmes Road

Map continues next page

For the other start points ignore the descent path and retrace the outward route to **Lockerbrook Farm**, from where to descend back to the car.

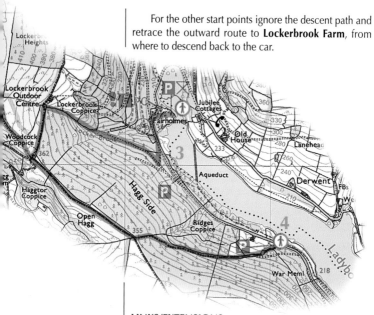

LINKS/EXTENSIONS

Link A

For a longer circular walk from start points 1 and 2, this route can be linked with Oyster Clough. After descending **The Tower**, walk roughly northwest below the big shale/rock cliff and cross the fence. Below and to the left there is a large plantation, above which a narrow path traverses the hillside. Follow the path and, once beyond the trees and a small stream, descend steeply as best you can to the **River Alport**. The idea is to ascend the steep slopes opposite (around SK 127 923) and cross the moorland above in a southwesterly direction (compass at the ready) to the upper reaches of **Oyster Clough** (SK 119 917). ◄ A good path contours back to join the Roman Road (SK 115 905), which can be followed northwest to Birchen Clough Bridge, or to Alport Bridge in the opposite direction.

The shooting cabin near the top of the clough contains a visitor's book and it can be nice to sit around here for a break.

ROUTE 23
Alport Castles Gully

The Tower provides a great photo opportunity once on the top

Start/Finish	Alport Bridge on A57, SK 142 896, Birchen Clough Bridge on A57, SK 109 913, Fairholmes Visitor Centre, SK 173 894 or lay-by on Fairholmes Road, SK 181 885
Height gain	50m
Grade and rating	2 (winter only)

This is one of several winter-only lines that could be climbed on this cliff: a shallow gully line, with a small rock step, cutting through the northern end of the big shale/rock cliff beyond The Tower. A period of frost and some snowfall are essential for this route to come into condition and, when frozen, the shale and grass provide good ice-axe placements. After heavy snow, care will be needed when walking above the cliff as cornices can form on the rim. It is also possible to complete a long traverse below the big rock band on this section of the cliff at a similar grade, and other lines exist on the right-hand section of the cliffs. In a good winter this route could be linked with a traverse of The Tower (Route 22).

Approach
As for Route 22, but continue northwest below the impressive cliff rather than heading for **The Tower**. The gully is near the northern end, just before the cliff and hillside merge.

See map for
Route 22 for rest
of route

Route
Climb steeply up a grassy slope (hopefully covered with snow) just to the right of a recess where big icicles often form. Work upwards to reach the rock band that forms the crux of the route. Ascend the short rock step into the shallow gully above and follow this to the top. Take extra care if a cornice has formed. Return to the start point as for Route 22.

KINDER SCOUT

This high moorland plateau contains the highest point in the Peak District (636m according to the map) and, in Kinder Downfall, one of its grandest spectacles. The whole area is very popular with walkers and often busy, especially at weekends and throughout the summer months. It is not quite so popular with rock climbers, although there is a guidebook to the gritstone edges and outcrops that surround the plateau (see Appendix B).

Ashop Clough with Nether Red Brook on the left and Upper Red Brook far right

The small village of Edale (or more properly Grindsbrook Booth), which lies in the valley below the southeastern edge of Kinder Scout, marks the southern end of the Pennine Way and the first of the many highlights of this long-distance path is the impressive waterfall known as Kinder Downfall, where the River Kinder tumbles into the ravine below on its way to Kinder Reservoir. This is a very popular objective and can be reached from several different start points, most of which are included in the following route descriptions. When in full flow, and at times of strong winds, the cascade presents a remarkable

Entering Fair Brook. Snow fills the line of Fairbrook Gully on the left with Fair Brook in the centre. Fairbrook Naze on skyline to the right

spectacle as the curtain of water is often blown back over the edge or sent soaring into the air above the ravine. In a good winter the waterfall freezes to provide a classic ice climb. This is a well-known occurrence and big queues can form at weekends, rather spoiling the experience.

The traditional routes onto Kinder Scout are well-trodden footpaths, which might contain a few small rock steps but do not require any scrambling skills. However, the following suggestions should make for a more inter-esting ascent, making use of the streambeds that fall from the plateau in most cases and including some prolonged, but not too serious, scrambling sections (except for those routes starting from the ravine of the River Kinder below the Downfall).

The 'Moors for the Future' project (see Introduction) is also busy on Kinder Scout and fencing is being erected here too. Consequently it will be necessary to seek out a suitable crossing point where the line of the fence crosses any of these routes. **Note** Kinder Scout was designated a National Nature Reserve in October 2009.

KINDER SCOUT NORTH AND ASHOP CLOUGH

Starting towards the eastern end of the northern edge of Kinder Scout there are several watercourses or gullies that fall from the edge of the plateau to join the River Ashop, which here runs alongside the A57 Snake Pass road. While some of these look from the road to be likely routes to the top, they are mostly quite overgrown and unwelcoming.

Ashop Clough lies further west and is hidden from the road, which turns north at this point, by the woodland of Snake Plantations. The clough is about 4.5km long and a good path runs along it all the way from the road to the western end of the Kinder Scout plateau near Mill Hill. Above the River Ashop, on its southern side, there are several more watercourses that fall from the plateau edge and some of these also provide an alternative way to reach the top. They are all accessed from the path alongside the river and the most significant and interesting have been included. Note that distances can be deceptive here, and what look like small boulders from the path assume a more massive presence at close quarters.

In a good winter, the north-facing slopes of Ashop Clough can hold snow for a long time, eventually forming nevé. Anyone wanting to practise long traverses across steep snow or even ice-axe arrests might have some fun here.

Starting towards the eastern end of the A57 Snake Pass road, the first route is Blackden Brook.

ROUTE 24

Blackden Brook

Start/Finish	Lay-by near Wood Cottage on A57, SK 130 895
Height gain	Main route 110m
	Alt finish 50m
Grade and rating	1 (summer and winter)
	Alt finish 1 (summer and winter) *

Blackden Brook (SK 128 890) is on every Peak District rambler's tick list and, when talking about scrambles in the Peak, the often-asked question is 'What about Blackden Brook?' Well... The walk alongside the stream is scenically impressive and leads into the steeper upper regions after passing a picturesque waterfall. However, one of the problems in trying to create a circular route taking in Blackden Brook is that a return will either involve a walk alongside the A57 (which is more dangerous than anything to be met on this scramble) or the need to descend the brook as well as ascend it. If two vehicles are used then this problem can be resolved; a link with Fair Brook (Route 25) being the most obvious.

In a really good winter a big ice pitch forms over some 'slabby' rocks on the left bank of the stream near the top, but this is really the preserve of ice climbers and it suffers from a lack of belays on the ground above, which is boggy. Mixed winter lines can be had in the rocks on the right or, in a really good winter, easy ice scrambling in the main watercourse. Since most of the scrambling interest lies at the top end of the brook, the alternative approach from the Edale side, given in the 'Links/extensions' section of Route 36, may be preferred.

The top section of the alternative finish

Approach

When you park in the lay-by near Wood Cottage watch the kerb clearance on your exhaust! If the suggested lay-by is full, there's a smaller one a little further on, just before a sharp right-hand bend (if driving from the Sheffield direction). Cross the nearby stile and take the path down the hillside towards Blackden Barn. Go across the footbridge and follow the path as it winds its way through the valley beside **Blackden Brook**. After about 1.5km, a large waterfall comes into sight on the left (marked on the map). Continue past this into a more rugged area where there is easier access to the streambed.

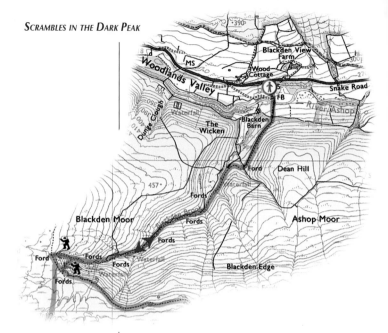

Route

As the clough becomes more defined and enclosed, follow the main streambed, clambering over boulders and small rock steps to reach a steeper section. This provides two or three further short rock steps before the plateau is reached.

Alternatively, just before the final steepening at the top of the brook (SK 118 883) there are two likely looking gully lines on the left that lead up the hillside to the plateau. The first (lowest down the brook) is more of a rock climb in its upper reaches, but the second provides a pleasant scramble. Cross the stream and move up a short grassy slope to clamber over boulders at first, following the line of the main watercourse where the rock is clean and sound. Eventually a corner is reached below a final steepening, which can be surmounted by an easy line on the right. Now move left and then easily up a steep little wall to the left of a short crack. Continue over boulders to join the path along the plateau.

From the top there are various options but they will all usually require a return to this spot for a descent of the brook back to the start point. The suggestion below provides a good walk and more scrambling before this becomes necessary.

LINKS/EXTENSIONS

Link A

Head due south across the short stretch of moorland to join the path overlooking Grindsbrook Clough (this used to be called the '10-minute crossing', which gives a clue as to how long it should take!). Follow this path westwards to reach the top of **Grindsbrook** (SK 106 876). Scramble down the streambed (reversing Route 35), to join the valley path back eastwards and follow this to the bottom of **Golden Clough** (SK 121 869).

Madwoman's Stones, (SK 137 880) a collection of weirdly eroded rocks about 750m to the east of the trig point, are worth a diversion on the way if energy levels are still high.

Take the path that leads up the side of the clough until it is possible to contour over to the foot of **Ringing Roger** (SK 125 871). Scramble up this broken ridge (see Route 36) and at the top walk a short distance to the left (west) back to the top of Golden Clough. From here, pick up the path that leads to the trig point (SK 129 878). Now head north across the plateau to reach the path along the edge and head west to descend **Blackden Brook** and return to the start point. ◀

ROUTE 25

Fair Brook

Start/Finish	Lay-by near the Snake Inn on A57, SK 113 905
Height gain	100m
Grade and rating	1 (summer and winter) *

This route involves a walk of about 2km to access easy scrambling over large 'slabby' rocks and short rock steps in the streambed leading to the plateau. The valley of Fair Brook is used by many as a route onto Kinder Scout from the A57 Snake Pass road, often for a crossing to Kinder Downfall. It is often completed as part of a circular walk, returning down Ashop Clough. Fairbrook Naze, situated above the upper western banks of the brook, is a prominent landmark when driving up the A57 from the Sheffield direction, especially in winter under a coating of snow. In a very cold winter ice can form for a considerable distance in the upper reaches of the brook, providing easy ice scrambling.

Approach

Park in one of the small lay-bys just below the Snake Inn on the A57. ▶ Cross the road and head southeastwards for a short distance to a stile. Climb over the stile into the woodland and follow the path (boggy in places) down to a footbridge over the **River Ashop** (SK 114 902). The path skirts around a steep nose at first and then follows the right bank of **Fair Brook** through picturesque scenery until, after about 2km, a level area is reached from where Fair Brook rises more steeply towards the plateau. While never far from the well-trodden footpath, the rocks provide a more absorbing way up this final stretch.

Parking is limited and an early start is usually a good idea, especially at weekends.

Route

Where the brook begins to steepen, join the streambed and choose a line to follow over boulders, slabs and short rock steps towards the top. Interest increases as the brook steepens even more near the top before eventually levelling off onto the plateau itself. A straightforward return can be made by following the path that runs along the edge of the plateau westwards, joining the **Pennine Way** for a short way to the top of **Ashop Clough** where it joins the **Snake Path** (SK 063 902). Follow the latter back east to the start point.

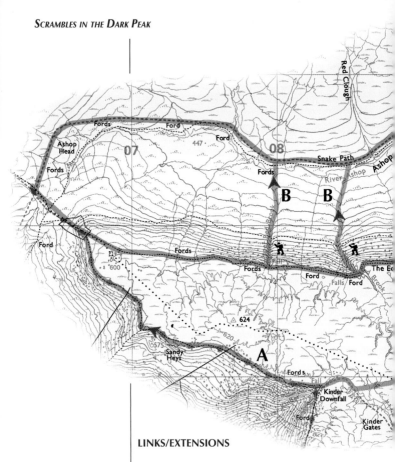

LINKS/EXTENSIONS

Link A

From the top of **Fair Brook** it is about 1km to **Kinder Downfall** 'as the crow flies', but many have got lost in the peat groughs between here and there! Heading a few degrees south of due west should result in meeting the broad sandy path (actually the bed of the River Kinder) that leads from Kinder Gates to the Downfall. Turn right (northwest) and follow the path (or the river when in full flow) to the Downfall. Follow the **Pennine**

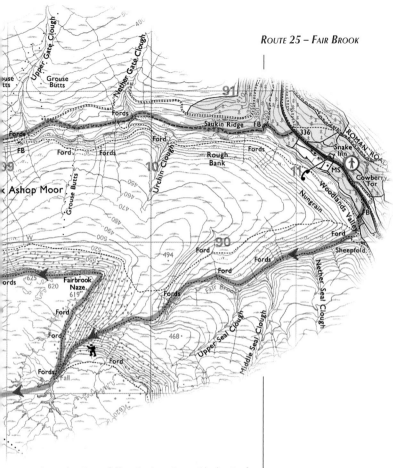

Way from the Downfall to its junction with the **Snake Path** (SK 063 902) and follow **Ashop Clough** back east to the A57.

Link B

If not visiting the Downfall, an alternative to the straightforward finish described for the main route is to follow the plateau edge westwards to descend one of the Red Brook options (either Route 27 or 28) into **Ashop Clough** and return to the start point along the **Snake Path**.

ROUTE 26
Fair Brook Gully

Start/Finish	Lay-by near the Snake Inn on A57, SK 113 905
Height gain	65m
Grade and rating	1 (summer and winter)

This route takes the line of the obvious shallow rocky gully on the hillside about 200m to the left of where the main Fair Brook streambed starts to rise to the plateau. It is steeper than it appears from below and after a scrappy start there are several better sections on more solid rock.

Approach
As for Route 25 to the level area.

Route
As the footpath enters the level area where **Fair Brook** begins its rise to the plateau, the grassy run-off from the gully can be seen rising from the left bank. Leave the path, descend to cross the brook and go up the grassy slope to the bottom of the route. Clamber through the initial broken section (loose in places) to a series of short rock steps. These lead to a steeper section that includes a short wall, avoided by moves on the right. Continue over good rock to the top where a path leads off to the right to the top of Fair Brook.

See map for Route 25 for rest of route

From here either follow the options in Route 25 or enjoy a very pleasant descent over the clean water-washed rocks of Fair Brook (reversing Route 25) before rejoining the main path back to the A57.

ROUTE 27

Nether Red Brook

Start/Finish	Lay-by near the Snake Inn on A57, SK 113 905 or car park at Birchen Clough Bridge, SK 109 914
Height gain	Main route 140m
	Alt finish 1 – 60m
	Alt finish 2 – 50m
Grade and rating	1 (summer and winter) **
	Alt finish 1: 3 (summer and winter)
	Alt finish 2: 1/2 (summer and winter)

This is the first of the routes in Ashop Clough, starting about 2.5km from the Snake Inn. Confusingly, the map shows two Nether Red Brooks. This route follows the most easterly of the two and offers enjoyable, easy scrambling over very clean water-washed gritstone with a number of short pitches to negotiate. The main streambed can be used as a descent.

Approach

Parking is limited and an early start is usually a good idea, especially at weekends.

The best option is to park in one of the small lay-bys just below the Snake Inn on the A57. ◄ Cross the road and walk northwestwards, passing the Snake Inn on the right. A few metres after the start of the woodland on the left, there is a stile (SK 110 907). Go over this and descend on the path to the **River Ashop**. Follow the path (Snake Path) over a footbridge and through the woods into **Ashop Clough**.

An alternative, useful when the lay-bys are full, is to use the small car park higher up the A57 at **Birchen Clough** Bridge (SK 109 914). Walking along the road can be dangerous, so the best option is to cross the road and follow the Forestry Commission's 'Forest Walk' path that starts opposite the car park. Follow this steeply down

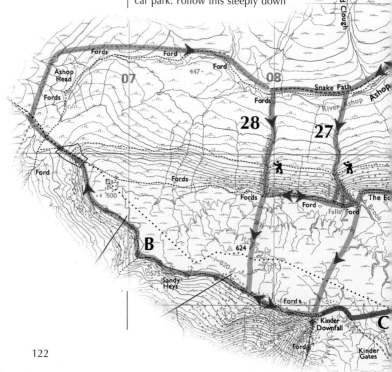

through the woods to a small stream. Keep to the left-hand (eastern) bank and drop down to a footbridge (the one mentioned above). Cross the footbridge and continue into **Ashop Clough**.

There follows a very nice walk by the side of the **River Ashop**, with the path rising and falling as it leads into more open moorland. Keep to the path until opposite the point where the first Nether Red Brook runs into the

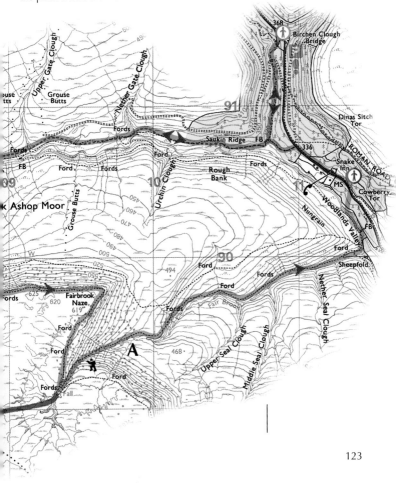

river (SK 085 904). The brook rises up the hillside, curving out of sight to the left as it nears the plateau edge, at which point two alternative finishing lines become visible. Cross the river to pick up a vague sheep track on the left-hand side of the brook. Follow this up the hillside to the steeper sections above.

Route

As soon as it appears worthwhile drop into the streambed and scramble over blocks and small falls into the steeper section. In summer, the water is soon left behind and the scrambling gets better on beautifully clean rock. Just before the brook begins to curve to the left a number of steeper steps must be negotiated – choose a line to suit for most interest. It is at this point that the previously mentioned alternatives for a finish come into play (described below). The main route continues to follow the streambed, which retains interest all the way to the top over several more sections of excellent water-washed rock.

Alternative finish 1 This is on the right, just before the main stream curves to the left. There is some loose, friable and greasy rock in the upper section and when wet the chimney at the top is extremely unpleasant, so it is best attempted only after a prolonged dry spell (if then!). Clamber over shattered rocks and boulders to a steep section of rock, climbed from right to left on a hidden ledge behind the initial rock wall. Continue over broken ground to reach the foot of a greasy corner. Care is needed here as much of the rock in this section is quite friable. Climb the corner to arrive below the deep and dirty chimney, making a careful exit to the left onto steep peat and heather ledges. Final moves over better rock lead to the top.

Alternative finish 2 Much more pleasant. It starts higher up the brook and around the curve from the first. Begin by clambering over boulders and shattered rock to reach a short steep wall. Climb this and then more boulders, which lead to a second rock step. Scramble over this and up to the foot of a wide chimney, climbed by a series of big ledges. Move over more blocks above to reach the top.

Climbing in the upper section of Nether Red Brook (Photograph: Chris Sleaford)

The wide chimney in the top section of alternative finish 2

Follow the path along the edge of the plateau westwards to the top of Upper Red Brook (Route 28) and descend back into **Ashop Clough** to return to the start point using the Snake Path.

LINKS/EXTENSIONS

Link A
Follow the path along the edge of the plateau eastwards to find the top of **Fair Brook** and descend the streambed (reversing Route 25) to meet the valley path for a return to the start point.

Link B
Cross the plateau in a southwesterly direction to join the **Pennine Way** to the west of Kinder Downfall. Head east to visit **Kinder Downfall** and then return towards **Mill Hill** to rejoin the **Snake Path** at its western end (SK 063 902) and follow this back to the start point.

Link C
As for Link B, but from Kinder Downfall cross the plateau northeastwards to the top of **Fair Brook** and reverse Route 25.

ROUTE 28
Upper Red Brook

Start/Finish	Lay-by near the Snake Inn on A57, SK 113 905 or car park at Birchen Clough Bridge, SK 109 914
Height gain	90m
Grade and rating	1 (summer and winter) *

Seen from the path by the River Ashop this is the next largest 'gash' in the edge of the plateau after Route 27. There is another Nether Red Brook marked on the map before Upper Red Brook is reached, but it holds little interest compared to its neighbours. This route has a more serious feel than Nether Red Brook (Route 27), but has fairly easy scrambling over large blocks and small rock pitches leading to a finish through rock outcrops on the edge of the plateau. Towards the top, the line taken will vary with prevailing conditions.

Approach
As for Route 27 but go past the bottom of both Nether Red Brooks, staying on the path by the **River Ashop** until near to where Upper Red Brook meets the river (SK 080 904). Cross the river and look for a vague sheep track on the left-hand side of the brook. Follow this up towards steeper ground.

Route
As soon as it seems worthwhile, drop into the watercourse and scramble over small steps and falls into steeper country. There is a shattered band of shale-like rock to negotiate but, once over this, things improve. Follow a line to suit over big blocks to below a short vertical wall, which

can be climbed on good holds in a crack system to the right of centre. Carry on over more blocks and follow a line trending leftwards near the top. Choosing a finish through the huge blocks here can be interesting, and the best option will depend on prevailing conditions. A corner over to the right is probably the easiest and can be found just beyond the obvious short chimney containing a chockstone (Ali's chimney). The chimney itself is steep but quite straightforward. ◄

Rucksacks may have to be removed to get under the chockstone, while those of a large girth are best avoiding it altogether!

Head back east along the plateau edge to Nether Red Brook (Route 27) and descend this back into **Ashop Clough** to return to the start point using the **Snake Path**.

LINKS/EXTENSIONS

Use any of the other links given under Route 27 (opting to visit the Downfall or not).

The tight chimney finish option to Upper Red Brook (Photograph: Chris Sleaford)

ROUTE 29
Far Upper Red Brook

Start/Finish	Lay-by near the Snake Inn on A57, SK 113 905 or car park at Birchen Clough Bridge, SK 109 914
Height gain	55m
Grade and rating	1 (summer and winter)

Not named on the map, this is the most westerly of our routes leading out of Ashop Clough onto the plateau. Situated to the west of Upper Red Brook, it gives a deceptively good little outing. At first glance it appears to be a non-starter but, on closer inspection, it proves to be a very pleasant line although shorter than the previous routes.

Approach

As for Routes 27 and 28 but continue up the **Snake Path** until it begins to turn to the right (SK 078 905). A track of sorts leads to the left and across the **River Ashop**. Faint sheep tracks can be used to work diagonally to the right and upwards towards the route, which is best entered (SK 074 902) before the ground begins to steepen. Even here its appearance is deceptive. Note that the line in this area that contains a deep gouge in the earth is *not* the one to aim for; it is the next one to the west.

Route

Clamber over boulders and up the streambed into the steeper section. Follow a series of short steps, taking as direct a line as possible on excellent rock. The path that follows the plateau edge cuts across the streambed near the top just as interest begins to wane, so this is a good place to stop.

Turn right (west) onto the path along the plateau edge and follow it to the junction with the **Pennine Way** (SK 067 899). Drop down the Pennine Way towards the junction with the **William Clough** path but, well before the junction and at about the 520m contour, move round to the left and follow a vague grassy path to find a short gully leading back up to the plateau through the first rock outcrops. This gives a short scramble at Grade 1/2 on rock that is a little loose at present. Rejoin the Pennine Way on top and head southeast to visit **Kinder Downfall**. From the Downfall head north across the plateau to descend one of the other Red Brook options (Routes 27 or 28) to the **Snake Path** and return to the start point.

LINKS/EXTENSIONS

Link A

From the Downfall head northeast to descend **Fair Brook** (Route 25).

Link B

A much shorter option. Turn left (east), walk along the plateau edge, and descend Route 27 or 28 for a return along the Snake Path.

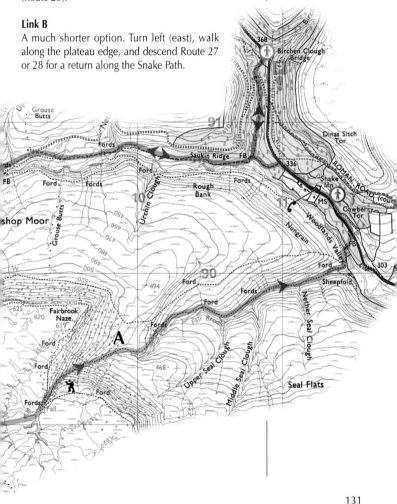

RIVER KINDER RAVINE

This is the deep ravine below Kinder Downfall through which flows the River Kinder after its tumble over the precipice from the plateau. From above it provides probably the grandest spectacle in the Dark Peak, but standing in its depths it can be an intimidating place. For the scrambler, there are three easily identifiable escape routes from high up in the ravine. All are at the top end of Grade 3 and demand respect. One of these, 'The Downfall Climb', is a classic 'Moderate' rock climb, only feasible in summer when the waterfall is virtually dry. In a good winter it provides a reasonable standard ice climb that, as noted previously, is on everyone's 'tick list' and suffers badly from crowds on winter weekends.

APPROACHES

There are several approaches to Kinder Downfall (SK 083 889) for the scrambler. The first option is best if only an ascent of the ravine routes or Red Brook (Routes 30–33) is desired. The next three options all provide a longer day with more scrambling content than the first one, but a descent into the ravine will be necessary to reach the start of the routes. The safest way of descent into the ravine from Kinder Downfall is to walk around the rim to reach the south side of the ravine and work down the easier slopes that lie beyond the rocks of Kinder Great Buttress (in the region of SK 082 885). For reasons of clarity, only the first (Bowden Bridge car park) approach to the ravine routes has been shown on the sketch map; likewise link routes that return to alternative start points are not shown. Users should consult the relevant route description for approaches and walks out if starting elsewhere.

From the **Hayfield** car park (c5km) at Bowden Bridge (SK 049 869) walk up Kinder Road and then follow the continuation path towards **Kinder Reservoir**. At the dam ignore the switchback to the left and take the lower path along the west side of the reservoir towards **William Clough** to reach a footbridge (SK 059 887). Cross the

footbridge and turn right onto the low-level path that leads to the eastern end of the reservoir, where the River Kinder runs into it (SK 064 884). Cross another footbridge here and follow a narrow path that leads along the riverbank, passing woodland and some beautiful waterfalls on the way to the bottom end of the River Kinder ravine. On a sunny summer's day this valley has to be one of the most beautiful in the Dark Peak. Follow the river all the way into the ravine and scramble over big rocks in the riverbed wherever possible until close to the bottom of the routes.

Traversing in from the bottom of the right hand corner of Kinder Downfall (Route 31)

Alternative approaches
From the **Snake Pass** (A57) use **Fair Brook** (Route 25: c4km) or either of the better routes from **Ashop Clough** (Route 27 or 28: c5km), followed by a crossing of the **Kinder Scout** plateau.

From the car park between **Upper** and **Barber Booth** follow **Crowden Clough** (Route 34: c5km) to the top and then continue on the well-worn path to **Kinder Downfall**, passing through Kinder Gates on the way.

From **Edale** follow the directions given for **Grindsbrook Clough** (Route 35: c6km). An ascent of **Ringing Roger** (Route 36) could be included, but that way is longer and will require a walk along the plateau edge to the top of Grindsbrook Clough to continue from there.

ROUTE 30
Square Chimney Exit

Start/Finish	Car park at Bowden Bridge, Hayfield, SK 049 869 (or alternatives)
Height gain	95m
Grade and rating	3 (summer and winter)

This comprises a series of short rock pitches with a few difficult moves, linked by broken ground, finishing with a chimney high above the ravine that leads to the plateau. The route is situated on the left-hand side of the ravine when facing the Downfall, and a little further up the ravine than Arpeggio Gully (Route 32) on the slopes opposite. It starts above an area marked by two very large, flattish boulders on the left of the streambed soon after the ground begins to steepen sharply. The route involves some moves at the rock-climbing grade of 'Difficult', and the use of a rope and protection is advised. All difficulties can be avoided by escaping onto steep grass if necessary, but that will bring its own problems!

Route

After scrambling through the big boulders in the riverbed (which is interesting when dry and clean) look for a fairly obvious line on the left above two very large, flat boulders. Clamber up over blocks to the first steepening in the form of a large slab with a flake overlap running down its middle. Climb the ramp on the right, moving left then up right to a steep corner. This pitch can be avoided by clambering over steep grass round to the right. Above, clean slabby rock leads to another steep pitch with a

shallow chockstone chimney. Move up this to a good ledge. Now either squirm under and up behind a large dubious-looking chockstone in the chimney on the left or, straight ahead, up a wide corner crack. Both ways lead to the steep grass and rocky slope above. Climb easily over one more rock step, then trend left towards the crags above heading for a corner high up on the left and capped by two chockstones. This is Square Chimney. Climb a short corner by the left wall to gain access to the chimney, which is best climbed on the left using back-and-foot technique

This leaves just a short walk up to the **Pennine Way** that runs along the edge.

To return to Bowden Bridge car park, follow the **Pennine Way** eastwards to **Kinder Downfall** and round to the southern rim of the ravine to descend **Red Brook** (Route 33) back to the **River Kinder** and on to the car park.

LINKS/EXTENSIONS

Link A
Follow the **Pennine Way** westwards and return by descending the **William Clough** path (SK 063 902).

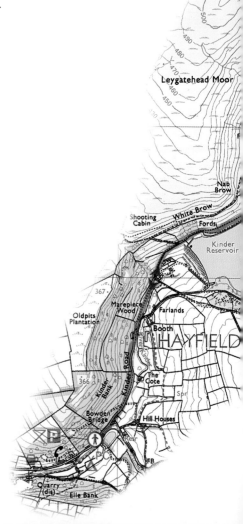

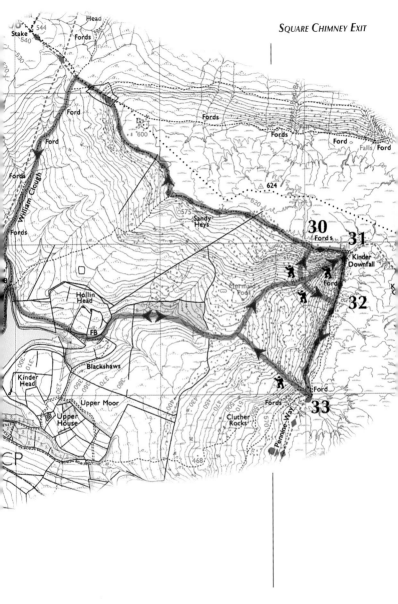

Above the first pitch. Easy work over water-washed slabs (Route 30)

ROUTE 31
Kinder Downfall Climb

Start/Finish	Car park at Bowden Bridge, Hayfield, SK 049 869 (or alternatives)
Height gain	50m
Grade and rating	3 (summer) 2/3 (winter) ***

This is the classic Kinder Scout summer and winter climb, graded 'Moderate' in the rock-climbing guidebook and deservedly given three stars. Sadly, it is not often in good climbable condition as this requires the waterfall to be dry, and it is not recommended at all if there is a flow of water. Despite its lowly climber's grade it is still a serious route and should be treated with respect. In a good winter, when the fall is frozen, the summer line provides an excellent ice climb, the popularity of which can result in queues at weekends. There is a more direct winter route, but that is strictly for the ice tyros.

Route

Scramble up the bed of the **River Kinder** over huge slabs and boulders to reach the foot of **Kinder Downfall**. The route starts in the bottom right corner of the wall and finishes at the top left, using a series of ledges and flakes with good holds. Start by climbing the right-hand corner and then moving diagonally upwards over ledges to the left, or traverse out left to begin with, move up and back to the right in the middle of the wall, and then trend up to the left to the finishing corner. ▶

Note that a helmet might be useful here to avoid getting brained by rocks dislodged by the sheep above (or even discarded bottles and cans from picnickers)!

Links/extensions

As for Route 30.

ROUTE 32
Arpeggio Gully

Start/Finish	Car park at Bowden Bridge, Hayfield, SK 049 869 (or alternatives)
Height gain	90m
Grade and rating	3 (summer) 2/3 (winter) ***

This route – good scrambling on clean, sound rock – is on the right-hand side of the ravine when facing Kinder Downfall and starts just a little lower down the ravine than Route 30 on the opposite hillside. It follows the obvious water-washed shallow gully line that leads almost all the way from the River Kinder to the plateau. In summer it is usually in climbable condition when the Downfall Climb is wet, and therefore offers an alternative ascent to save the day for the more resolute scrambler. There is more continuous rock here than in Route 30 and a steep section near the top has a quite serious feel to it. With one or two moves at the rock-climbing grade of 'Difficult', the use of a rope and protection is recommended.

Route

Scramble over big boulders in the bed of the **River Kinder** until the clean water-washed line of Arpeggio Gully is reached on the right. Scramble easily up blocks to the first steep rock pitch. This can be avoided by taking to steep grass on the right. Now follow a series of short rock steps to arrive at a corner with small chockstones in the cracks to the left and straight ahead. Move up using a combination of these and continue more easily to another steep corner under a small overhang. Step up to the right and use a series of small ledges and cracks to

Looking down the steep top section of Arpeggio Gully

reach easier ground above. Alternatively move off to the left over rocks and grass. Easy moves over more blocks lead to the top.

LINKS/EXTENSIONS
As for Route 30.

ROUTE 33
Red Brook

Start/Finish	Car park at Bowden Bridge, Hayfield, SK 049 869 (or alternatives)
Height gain	150m
Grade and rating	1 (summer and winter) **

Yes, another Red Brook! It joins (SK 075 884) the River Kinder after flowing down the hillside to the right (east) where the ravine begins to open up. It is good in ascent or descent between the River Kinder and the plateau above and provides a long, easy scramble with many short pitches on excellent water-washed rock. A covering of snow and/or ice makes for a good day out in winter.

Approach
See the main approach route described in 'Approaches' at the start of this section. About 250m after leaving the woods on the path by the river, look for the bottom of **Red Brook** running down the slopes to the right. ▶

In summer the entry into these lower reaches of the watercourse can be a tedious slog through dense bracken.

Route
As soon as possible enter the streambed and get involved with the rock. The lower section will carry some spring water in summer. Small waterfalls and one big one, which can be easily avoided, lead into the higher reaches of the brook, which is usually dry in summer. Interest increases above halfway as the course of the brook narrows down and gets steeper, providing a succession of pitches over beautiful rock slabs and short walls that lead to the top, where a final short wall ends on the path along the top of the ravine.

Turn left along the plateau edge and walk north to **Kinder Downfall**. From there, follow the **Pennine Way** northwestwards to the top of the **William Clough** path (SK 063 902) and descend this to return to Bowden Bridge car park via Kinder Reservoir.

LINKS/EXTENSIONS
As for Route 30, but also consider these options.

Link A
On the way to Kinder Downfall, descend into the ravine to climb one of the routes from there (Routes 30–32) back to the plateau.

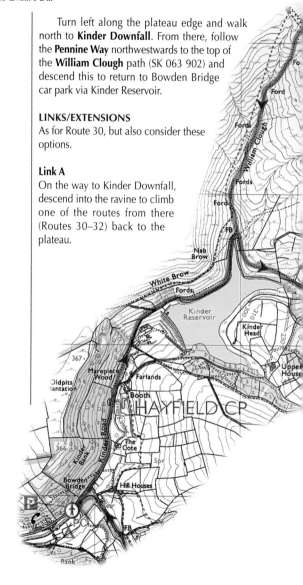

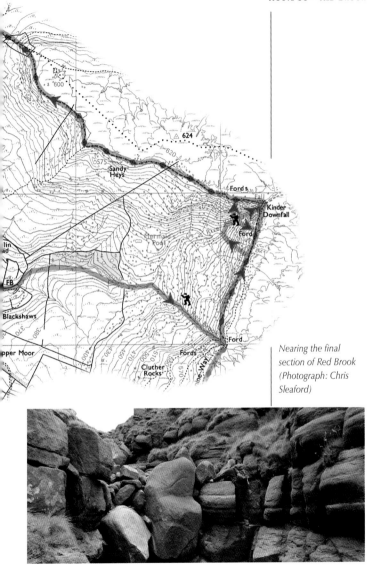

*Nearing the final
section of Red Brook
(Photograph: Chris
Sleaford)*

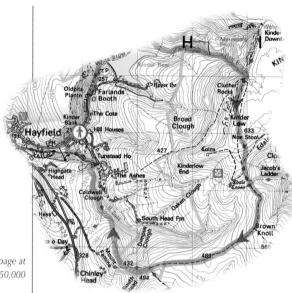

Map on this page at 1:50,000

Link B

To return to the Bowden Bridge car park, an interesting, but quite long, circular walk (c8km) can be made by following the **Pennine Way** south over **Kinder Low**. Continue southwards and where the Pennine Way swings to the east (SK 081 862) to descend Jacob's Ladder go straight on to reach the path that runs by a wall towards **Brown Knoll** (SK 084 851). Follow this path and, ignoring the fork to the left (SK 081 854) for Brown Knoll, continue southwesterly to **South Head** (SK 061 845). Go steeply over this and follow the path over **Mount Famine** (SK 056 849). Continue to follow the ridge line, descending eastwards on the path (SK 051 864) to the south of the plantation near **Stones Houses** to follow a good path northwestwards to the car park, or go a little further south and drop down onto the bridleway (SK 054 862) that runs back north past **Tunstead House** to the car park.

Looking down the beautiful water-washed rock in the mid section of Red Brook

KINDER SCOUT SOUTH

Probably the most popular, hence busy, side of Kinder Scout, the area includes the official starting point of the Pennine Way – The Nag's Head pub at Grindsbrook Booth. The path has been re-routed over to Jacob's Ladder, which gives access to firmer ground underfoot along the western edge of the plateau as opposed to its previous course through the peat bogs from the top of Grindsbrook or Crowden Clough to Kinder Downfall. However, the paths up the latter two cloughs remain well trodden, especially during summer weekends and school holidays. Most visitors keep to the footpaths, whereas these routes add some easy scrambling in the steepening streambeds as they rise to the plateau. An ascent of Ringing Roger gives a more exciting alternative to Golden Clough in reaching the path around Kinder Scout's southern edge.

The first scrambling section in Crowden Clough

ROUTE 34
Crowden Clough

Start/Finish	Car park near railway bridge between Barber Booth and Upper Booth, SK 107 847
Height gain	150m
Grade and rating	1 (summer) 1/2 (winter) **

This is a very popular walking route onto Kinder Scout. The path follows the course of Crowden Brook all the way to the top but it is possible, at about two thirds of the way along, to take to the streambed for a more interesting boulder-hopping variation. There are several good scrambling sections and an optional finish through the rock outcrop at the very top of the brook, which can involve a tight squeeze for those of a larger frame! An excellent day out at any time of the year, especially so during a prolonged cold snap when the upper reaches of the brook can freeze to form one particularly good ice pitch and a few shorter stretches of 'ice scrambling' towards the top.

Approach
Park in the car park situated just past the railway bridge on the road between **Barber Booth** and Upper Booth. Walk up the road to **Upper Booth** and, just across a bridge and on the right, cross a stile to follow a path into the start of Crowden Clough (SK 103 853). The path gradually gains height as it wends its way along the side of **Crowden Brook**.

Route
After about 2.5km the path heads steeply up the left-hand bank towards the rock-climbing crag of **Crowden Tower**.

This is where the fun begins! Ignore the path and stay low to enter the watercourse and follow it to the first short section of scrambling where the brook falls three or four metres over a series of ledges. Continue in the same vein to reach a second, steeper scrambling section above a small pool (often dry in summer). Climb this by using small steps in the back corner at first and then choosing a more or less direct line above this (in a hard winter this is the good ice pitch).

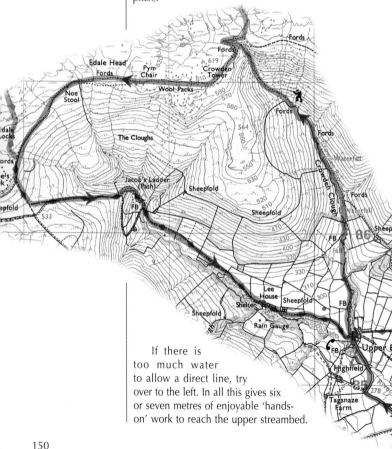

If there is too much water to allow a direct line, try over to the left. In all this gives six or seven metres of enjoyable 'hands-on' work to reach the upper streambed.

Continue to follow the streambed over one or two more rock steps towards the top and the path that runs along the southern edge of Kinder Scout. At the top, rather than joining the path straight away, purists may opt to prolong the scrambling experience by continuing along the streambed to the final rock outcrop, where a choice of chimneys can be climbed onto the plateau. The one to the right is probably easiest, but still a Grade 2 'thrutch' that can be a struggle if wearing a rucksack or of larger than average build! Options from here are given below.

Nearing the top of the second scrambling section

151

To return, follow the path along the plateau edge to the west for a descent of the **Jacob's Ladder** path (SK 081 862) back to **Upper Booth** and on to the start point.

LINKS/EXTENSIONS

Link A

For a longer day (c4km), walk back to the right (eastwards) to join the path (SK 095 873) northwards to **Kinder Downfall**, passing the rock formation of Kinder Gates (SK 088 887) on the way. An option here is to descend into the **River Kinder** ravine to complete one of the routes there (Routes 30–32).

From the Downfall, follow the **Pennine Way** south along the edge, over **Kinder Low** (SK 079 870) and descend **Jacob's Ladder** to return to the start point.

Looking down the second section of scrambling in Crowden Clough

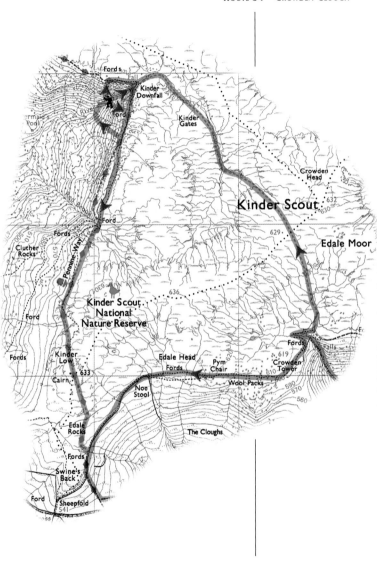

ROUTE 35
Grindsbrook Clough

Start/Finish	Car park near Edale Station, SK 124 853
Height gain	75m
Grade and rating	1 (summer and winter) *

Grindsbrook from Upper Tor, with the normal finish rising up the slope in the background

This is as equally popular a route onto Kinder Scout as Crowden Clough (Route 34): a straightforward walk and some easy clambering in the streambed leads to better scrambling over blocks, slabs and ledges in a deep ravine to reach the top. Scrambling interest is confined to the very last section, where the streambed rears up steeply as it cuts into the plateau to give an excellent finish on clean water-washed rock. The route can also be used as an alternative to the usual path alongside Grinds Brook for a descent into the valley bottom.

Approach

Park in the pay-and-display car park near **Edale Station**. Walk northwards through the village to pick up the start of the footpath (SK 122 861) on the right not far after the famous Nag's Head pub (the official start point of the Pennine Way). The path leads into Grindsbrook Clough and gains height gradually, following the course of the brook until after about 3km it begins to climb more steeply towards the plateau. A little further on (SK 106 873) the path leads straight ahead up a rocky section onto the plateau.

Route

Do not go straight ahead. Instead, follow the brook round to the right, where the main streambed plunges off the plateau and down a rocky ravine. Choose a line up the ravine on a mixture of fallen slabs and boulders at first, followed by a series of short rock steps and large flat ledges leading to the top. Soon after entering the ravine there is a steep gully rising to the left that offers easy scrambling (Grade 1/2, 30m), but the main ravine is more enjoyable, entertaining and longer, with some great views back from above halfway.

155

Follow the path along the plateau edge to the east, passing **Upper Tor** (SK 115 876) and Nether Tor (SK 122 875). For extra scrambling, after Upper Tor cross the plateau (north) to descend the upper section of **Blackden Brook** (Route 24) to the point where the harder alternative finish begins and ascend this back to the top before recrossing the plateau to rejoin the main path. After Nether Tor, head south to descend **Ringing Roger** (Route 36) and rejoin the **Grinds Brook** path back to **Edale**.

LINKS/EXTENSIONS

Link A
Walk back southwards from the top of the ravine to rejoin the original path (SK 105 872) from **Edale**. Continue round the edge to the top of **Crowden Brook** and pick up Route 34 and the links from there.

Crowden Clough–Grindsbrook Clough circuit
The classic walking route hereabouts is a round of the full southern edge of the plateau. However, combining the ascent of Crowden Clough with a descent of Grindsbrook Clough, with or without a visit to **Kinder Downfall**, will give an alternative day out with plenty of 'hands-on' content. The re-routed **Pennine Way** runs between **Grindsbrook Booth** (SK 123 859) and **Upper Booth** (SK 103 854) so a circuit in either direction is possible, but Crowden Clough is best in ascent from a scrambling point of view.

ROUTE 36
Ringing Roger

Start/Finish	Car park near Edale Station, SK 124 853
Height gain	40m
Grade and rating	1/2 (summer and winter)

Ringing Roger (SK 125 871) sits high above Grindsbrook and consists of a series of small rock outcrops set one above the other to form a sort of broken ridge climbing the hillside to the Kinder Scout plateau. The position is excellent, providing good views into the upper reaches of Grindsbrook Clough as height is gained. The route offers short sections of easy scrambling over a series of small outcrops leading to grassy slopes at the top; the grading reflects the fact that a harder line can be taken by seeking out problems on the way up. Though not very long, and easily escapable, the route provides an interesting diversion on the way to the plateau above.

Competitive scramblers could have fun trying to outdo each other here!

Approach
Start as for Grindsbrook Clough (Route 35). Soon after leaving the road in **Grindsbrook Booth** – and just as the first section of woodland on the left is being passed – a path begins (SK 123 863) to lead off upwards to the right over Heardman's Plantation.

Route
Follow the path as it zigzags uphill and out of sight towards **The Nab**. At a fork in the path (SK 125 866) take the left uphill turn and follow this path until it begins to

level out beneath the rocks of **Ringing Roger** itself. Work up to the foot of the first outcrop, where the hardest line is directly up the centre of the wall. Climb the subsequent small buttresses and ledges until the final one is dealt with. Any difficulty can be avoided to the left of the direct line.

At the top, follow a minor path to the left to join (SK 125 875) the main one leading to the top of **Golden Clough** and the plateau. Follow the path to the west, with great views all the way, to arrive at the top of Grindsbrook Clough (SK 106 876). Descend the ravine (reversing Route 35) to return to the valley path and the start point.

Add in more scrambling by heading north across the plateau shortly after passing **Nether Tor** (SK 121 876) to join the northern edge path. Turn west upon reaching it and walk to the top of **Blackden Brook** (SK 116 884). Descend the top section of the brook (Route 24) to

Ringing Roger (second ridge back) from Upper Tor

the point where the alternative finish begins and ascend this back to the plateau. Cross back to the southern edge and follow the path westwards to the top of Grindsbrook Clough to continue as above.

In all, this gives four contrasting lines of ascent and descent with several interesting viewpoints.

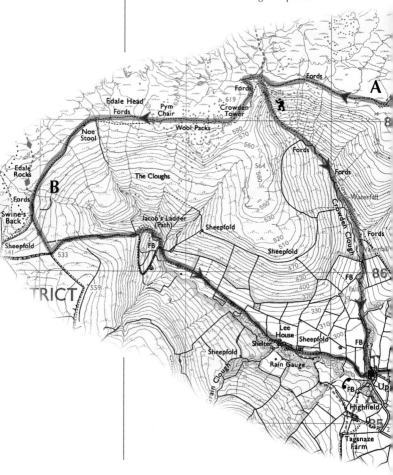

LINKS/EXTENSIONS

Link A

Continue along the path round the edge to descend Crowden Clough. Return on the **Pennine Way** between Upper Booth and Edale as described in the Crowden Clough–Grindsbrook Clough Circuit (above).

Link B

As above but stay on the path to go past Crowden Tower to rejoin the **Pennine Way** and return down the **Jacob's Ladder** path to Upper Booth and Edale.

There are some other options remaining in the Edale Valley, but they are limited as far as scrambling content goes. The following offer a little sport.

Jaggers Clough (SK 154 874)

At the top of the clough there is a short section of boulder scrambling in the streambed with one small waterfall. It seems little return for a long walk, although it is not as well trodden as other Kinder Scout cloughs and there are good views to be had during its ascent. It leads to the path that runs around the whole of the plateau edge.

Grain Clough (SK 095 854)

This and the unnamed clough above Dale Head (SK 099 842) contain too much vegetation to be of interest in summer, but when clothed in winter snow they can provide an alternative (but inferior) excursion to the bigger things described on previous pages.

OUTLYING AREAS

Away from the moors of the Dark Peak there are other scrambling opportunities, some of which are very good indeed. The next three routes (Routes 37–39) are well known to local climbers and are regularly climbed.

ROUTE 37
Back Tor Gully

Start/Finish	Odin Mine on old A625, SK 135 835 or Edale Station, SK 124 853
Height gain	60m
Grade and rating	2/3 (winter only) *

This is the obvious gully line (SK 146 851) on the northern side of Back Tor, which lies on the Mam Tor–Lose Hill ridge. It is well known to climbers who come here in good winters to frighten themselves on its steep northern face, which is perhaps only slightly less scary than the open face of Mam Tor. Crampons and axes are essential, and the use of a rope is recommended. The route can only be recommended after some snowfall and a long frosty spell, when the shale and grass are bound together.

Approach
There are two possibilities. 1) From the Castleton side, park near the disused Odin Mine on the old A625 road. Walk up the road until near **Mam Farm** (SK 133 840) then go over a stile and up northeastwards to **Hollins Cross** (SK 136 845) on the ridge. Once there follow the ridge eastwards until just before the path steepens to climb up

Back Tor. Leave the path and find a way as best you can over ankle-straining terrain below the north face to find the obvious gully line towards the left hand (eastern) end of the buttress.

2) From the Edale side, having parked at **Edale Station** (SK 124 853) or arrived by train, a path leaves the valley road near Yeman's Bridge (SK 123 852) and leads up to the back of **Mam Tor** in one direction, or to Hollins Cross in the

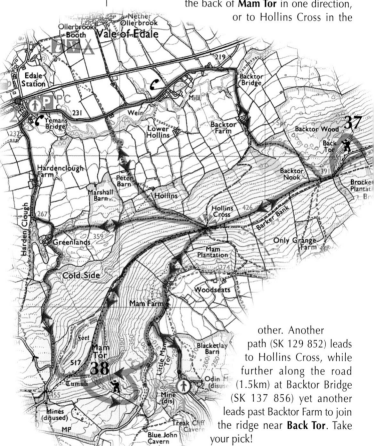

other. Another path (SK 129 852) leads to Hollins Cross, while further along the road (1.5km) at Backtor Bridge (SK 137 856) yet another leads past Backtor Farm to join the ridge near **Back Tor**. Take your pick!

Route

Having arrived below the line of the gully, climb steep grass (preferably frozen with snow on top) to reach the rock band at the base of the gully proper. Climb this to get into the 'scoop' above. An erosion runnel can be used to reach more rocks just below the top. Either climb a steep corner above, or move left and up on easier ground, to reach the summit.

Return the way you came or, if fitness levels are high and conditions are really good, a walk back westwards along the ridge leads to **Mam Tor**, where a descent of the southeast ridge and a traverse back into the shadow of the main face will enable an ascent of Mam Tor Gully (Route 38) as well. Even if the gully is not an objective, it is well worth walking back this way just to 'bag' the summit of Mam Tor before returning to the car.

The winter gully line on Back Tor

ROUTE 38

Mam Tor Gully

Start/Finish	Odin Mine on old A625, SK 135 835 or Edale Station, SK 124 853
Height gain	About 70m depending on conditions
Grade and rating	1 (winter only) ***

This has to be another classic. Climbing up the obvious gully/depression towards the left of the open face of Mam Tor (SK 129 835) this line is truly impressive for the Peak District and very satisfying to view from a distance thinking smugly 'I've done that'. A period of hard frost and a sprinkling of snow are absolutely essential to bring the route into condition. As the route faces eastwards, these conditions only persist in a really hard winter. Even so, an early start when it is still cold is always a good idea. Crampons and ice axes are essential and the use of a rope will help boost confidence. If the sun is warm, stones may roll down from the steep rocks above the gully and over to the right (truly Alpine!) so the wearing of a helmet is recommended.

When the snow is deep, wiser heads may like to delay their ascent a little to allow the keener types to produce a line of steps all the way up. If the gully line is not in condition, or appears unattractive, a walk up the southeast ridge provides an alternative way to reach the summit. Inevitably, other lines have been climbed on the face but they are not for the ice scrambler, more for the slightly insane!

Approach

As for Route 37. If parked near the disused Odin Mine, walk up the old road for most interest until it is possible

Mam Tor with the winter-only gully line picked out by light snow

to work up the slope to the bottom of the gully. If coming from the Edale side or from **Hollins Cross** along the ridge, a careful descent of the southeast ridge followed by a short traverse northwards will arrive below the gully line.

Route
The slope below the gully steepens to a short step, which may halt progress. Choose a line to suit, the aim being to get into the gully/depression above. From here, if you are lucky, follow steps made by previous parties up the gully. As the slope steepens near the top, trend leftwards towards rocks and break out onto the ridge not far from the summit.

If fitness levels are high and conditions are really good, a walk eastwards along the ridge to climb **Back Tor** Gully (reversing Route 37 extension) could be considered.

ROUTE 39

Elbow Ridge

Start/Finish	Roadside on old A625 (SK 139 829) or Speedwell Cavern pay-and-display car park (SK 139 828)
Height gain	65m
Grade and rating	3 (summer and winter) ***

Situated (SK 135 826) at the eastern end of Winnats Pass and on limestone for a change, this is a great route in the form of a proper ridge in a classic setting. It is a great way to start the classic walk (c10km including the climb) that incorporates the Mam Tor–Lose Hill ridge: a fairly steep first section leading to easier scrambling with increasing exposure towards the top. However, it is graded 'Difficult' in rock climbers' guidebooks, so a rope and some protection may help boost confidence; and as limestone can be slippery even when dry, it is probably best avoided when wet or damp.

An important note regarding the sensitive issue of access: this is National Trust land and, because the ridge is so close to the road with the possibility of rocks being dislodged onto vehicles or people passing below, the BMC website suggests that any ascents are made midweek, early or late in the day, and only in very small parties. This seems like sound advice, which should be adhered to.

Approach

Park on the old main road (SK 139 829) that leads to the disused Odin Mine, from where a short path leads into the rear of the **Speedwell Cavern** pay-and-display car park (SK 139 828). Go through the car park and into

the bottom end of **Winnats Pass**. The route takes the first obvious ridge line on the right (north), which starts near the roadside and climbs past a horizontal section in an almost unbroken line to the top.

Elbow Ridge at the bottom end of Winnats Pass

Route

The first section is the hardest but it can be avoided up steep grass on either side. The horizontal section that follows is fun and, under snow, crawling or an excruciating *à cheval* may be the best technique for many. Scramble up the continuation ridge to the top, with increasing exposure. To return from here, descend the slopes back east towards the bottom of the pass to return to the start point. For the full 10km circuit, from the top of the climb, take a path westwards to the top of **Winnats Pass** and at Winnats Head Farm (SK 131 829) turn north to take the path to join the old road (SK 131 833). Across the road a path leads up the southeastern ridge of **Mam Tor** to the top.

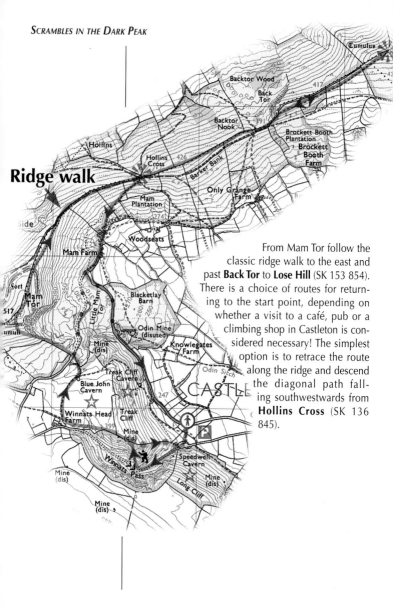

Ridge walk

From Mam Tor follow the classic ridge walk to the east and past **Back Tor** to **Lose Hill** (SK 153 854). There is a choice of routes for returning to the start point, depending on whether a visit to a café, pub or a climbing shop in Castleton is considered necessary! The simplest option is to retrace the route along the ridge and descend the diagonal path falling southwestwards from **Hollins Cross** (SK 136 845).

ROUTE 40

Roaches Lower and Upper Tier Ridges

Start/Finish	Lay-by below The Roaches, SK 004 621
Height gain	n/a
Grade and rating	1, 2 or 3 (summer) *

The Roaches (grid square SK 00 62), just off the A53 Leek-to-Buxton road, is often used as a starting point for a circular walk taking in The Roaches skyline, Ramshaw Rocks and Hen Cloud. Including this route will give an exciting start! In older rock-climbing guides the lower ridge was graded 'Moderate' with a one-star rating at a length of 500 feet (160m). The rock can feel sandy at times, but being rough gritstone a suitable line can usually be found even after rain. The lower ridge is really a long series of boulder problems, while the upper ridge is more varied with a number of slabs and narrow chimneys or grooves leading to a finish behind the top of the famous Whillans/Brown rock climb, The Sloth. The choice of line taken will determine the difficulties met, hence the spread of gradings given above. There are great views in all directions from the top of the Upper Tier Ridge.

Approach

Turn off the A53 Leek-to-Buxton road where signposted for Upper Hulme and follow this minor road as it twists its way through the village. After about 1.5km, park in one of the lay-bys below **The Roaches** which will be visible on the skyline above. A narrow gate gives access to a path running up the hillside. Follow the path over to the right, making for the very end of the lower-tier rocks.

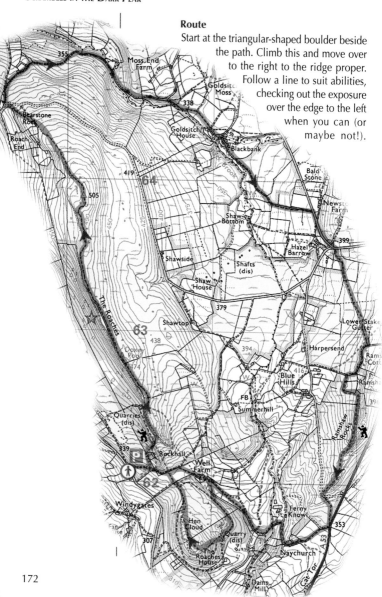

Route

Start at the triangular-shaped boulder beside the path. Climb this and move over to the right to the ridge proper. Follow a line to suit abilities, checking out the exposure over the edge to the left when you can (or maybe not!).

Approaching the crack and chimney towards the end of the upper tier ridge

Some of the holds are quite rounded but there is plenty of friction to be had on the rough gritstone. Eventually the route peters out onto the ground above. From here, follow a path leading diagonally downhill and to the right to arrive at the right-hand end of the Upper Tier Ridge. Move around to the right where slabby rocks lead easily to a narrow chimney/gully on the right-hand flank. Climb this onto a sloping slab.

Either drop down over the back of the slab into a tunnel through the rocks and find your way back to daylight over to the right or, harder, walk up to the top right of the slab, drop over the edge onto a chockstone and carefully work your way down the short chimney (back and foot technique is useful). Either way arrives at the same place. More slabby rocks lead to a short crack below another chimney/groove, which is more easily climbed to the right or, harder, straight ahead and over the top. Further slabs lead easily to the top, ending just beyond and behind the top of the Sloth.

To return from here, take the good path leading around the southern end of the rocks back to the start point. Otherwise, a classic 10km circuit, taking in Ramshaw Rocks and Hen Cloud is possible from the top of the upper ridge. A well-trodden path along the top of the main rock buttresses (the so-called 'Roaches Skyline Walk') leads northeast to Roach End and a minor road just beyond (SJ 996 645). There are excellent views and (for the keen types) more scrambly bouldering opportunities en route. Drop down the path leading northeast into the valley of Black Brook and turning eastwards to pass **Goldsitch House** (SK 009 643) and **Blackbank**, aiming to meet the minor road again near **Newstone Farm** (SK 017 638). Turn right along the road and after about 250m, near a road junction (SK 018 636), take the path leading south across the moorland to **Ramshaw Rocks**, which rear up prominently on the skyline.

While at **Ramshaw Rocks**, much fun can be had on the slabs to the rear of the crag. The central section in particular forms a kind of ridge with slabby rocks and deep wide cracks on the western side and sheer drops over the edge of the crag to the east. The slabs can be linked together to form a traverse of sorts, with difficulties to be had at Grades 1–3 on excellent rock. It is probably better to walk past the whole ridge and then climb it from the lower, southern end, starting at a slab with the letters 'DFC' scored on it. Work up wide cracks to open ground and a 'beckoning' finger pinnacle. Harder variations are possible by keeping to the left, but the easiest line is up a shallow ramp leading round to the right onto the exposed east face and then up through a chimney/crack on the left. A series of wide cracks, chimneys and slabs can now be used for the remaining traverse. Choose a line to suit ability, staying on the left side of the ridge. ◄

If taken north to south the route would be more difficult as it is mostly descent all the way.

From Ramshaw Rocks follow the path down to **Naychurch** (SK 015 616) and either return to **The Roaches** and the start point, or take the concessionary path (SK 010 620) near **Well Farm** and head up to **Hen Cloud**. Follow the contour path leftwards into the trees to meet another path heading diagonally up right past old quarried rock to the summit. Explore the rocks down 'Easy Gully' or head northwards back down towards The Roaches and the car.

ROUTE 41
Chrome Hill/Parkhouse Hill

Start/Finish	Earl Sterndale (near church: SK 091 671)
Height gain	75m/60m
Grade and rating	1 (summer and winter)

Parkhouse Hill (SK 078 668) and Chrome Hill (SK 071 673) are situated close to the villages of Earl Sterndale and Hollinsclough and offer easy scrambling over their two tops best enjoyed by traversing the two summits from the west. In wet or damp conditions the limestone outcrops are very slippery and great care should be taken if deciding to scramble over them as the adjoining slopes are very steep and a fall could be difficult to halt. In winter, under a covering of snow, they can provide good sport and it is recommended that full winter gear be carried in case conditions on arrival warrant it.

There is a concessionary path onto Chrome Hill and access onto Parkhouse Hill, a problem for many years, is now possible as a result of the CROW Act. However, it is important that visitors stay on the signed access paths until reaching open country.

Approach

The starting point will depend on where parking can be found and so the plan for the day needs to be flexible. If you can't park in **Earl Sterndale**, try **Hollinsclough** or, a little further away, **Longnor**.

Route

Park in **Earl Sterndale** and pick up the path that runs from behind the 'Quiet Woman' pub (SK 090 670) to descend

Parkhouse Hill's west ridge showing the short scrambling sections

westwards through fields to join the B5053 road (SK 084 688). Cross the road and continue on the path passing below Parkhouse Hill and on to **Glutton Grange Farm** (SK 084 670) to the northeast. The path turns to the west for a short distance, then north through a narrow valley to a junction of paths (SK 082 677).

Follow the path to the west for about 600m to join the minor road running through **Dowel Dale** and follow this towards **Stoop Farm** (SK 064 681). Turn up the Stoop Farm access track to find a sign-posted concessionary path that leads to the north-western end of **Chrome Hill**. Follow the path up the ridge, taking in whichever short scrambling sections appeal, to the summit from where there are great views to all points of the compass.

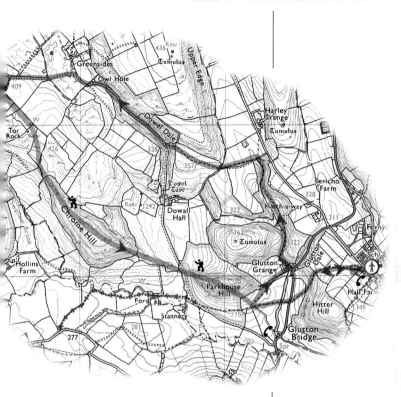

Descend the southeast ridge to a minor road (SK 076 670). Cross the road and go to the right of the prominent pinnacle (which could be included by keener types, although it is quite steep) to find the path leading up **Parkhouse Hill**'s west ridge. Follow the ridge, which has several short scrambling sections, to the summit.

Descend the east ridge back to the B5053 and return on the uphill path back to Earl Sterndale.

APPENDIX A
Index of routes

APPENDIX B
Further reading

Baker, Ernest A *Moors, Crags and Caves of the High Peak and Neighbourhood* (Heywood, (London 1903; 2nd facsimile edition, Halsgrove 2002)

Brown, Joe *The Hard Years* (Gollancz, London 1967)

Byne, Eric and Sutton, Geoffrey *High Peak* (Secker & Warburg, London 1966)

Collier, Ron (with Roni Wilkinson) *Dark Peak Aircraft Wrecks Vol 1* (Wharncliffe Books, Barnsley, 2nd revised edition 1995)

Dark Peak Aircraft Wrecks Vol 2 (Wharncliffe Books, Barnsley, 2nd revised edition 1992)

Milburn, Geoff (Ed) *Peak District Climbs: Fourth Series Vol 6, Moorland Gritstone Chew Valley* (BMC, 2001)

Peak District Climbs, Fifth Series Vol 2, Moorland Gritstone Kinder and Bleaklow (BMC, 1990)

Monkhouse, Patrick *On foot in the Peak* (Maclehose & Co, London 1932)

Rothman, Benny *The 1932 Kinder Trespass* (Willow Publishing, Altrincham 1982)

Smith, Roland 'Forgive us our Trespassers' (contained in *The Seven Blunders of the Peak* Brian Robinson [Ed]) (Scarthin Books, Cromford 1994)

Stainforth, Gordon *The Peak Past and Present* (Constable, London 1998)

APPENDIX C
Useful contacts

Accommodation
Peak District online (all types of
accommodation)
info@peakdistrictonline.co.uk
Tel: 08455 166 8022

Peak District Tourist Board
www.visitpeakdistrict.com

The Moorland Visitor Centre
Fieldhead
Edale
Hope Valley S33 72A
Tel: 01433 670207
edale@peakdistrict.gov.uk

Tourist Information Centres
Leek TIC
1 Market Place
Leek
Staffordshire ST13 5HH
Tel: 01538 483741
tourism.services@staffsmoorlands.gov.uk

Saddleworth Museum TIC
High Street
Uppermill
Saddleworth
Oldham OL3 6HS
Tel: 01457 870336
eca.saddleworthtic@oldham.gov.uk

Travel
peak.connections@peakdistrict.gov.uk

Train services
Tel: 0845 00 00 1125
www.northernrail.org

Traveline tel: 0871 200 2233
http://traveline.info

Other contacts
Aircraft wrecks in the Peak District
(there are many others)
www.peakdistrictaircrashes.co.uk

British Mountaineering Council
177–179 Burton Road
Manchester M20 2BB
www.theBMC.co.uk

Mountain Rescue
www.mountain.rescue.org.uk
Emergency SMS Website (to register
your mobile phone)
www.emergencysms.org.uk

Mountain Weather Information Service
www.mwis.org.uk

Natural England (East Midlands region)
Endcliffe
Deepdale Business Park
Ashford Road
Bakewell
Derbyshire DE45 1GT
www.naturalengland.org.uk

Peak District National Park Authority
Aldern House
Baslow Road
Bakewell
Derbyshire DE45 1AE
www.peakdistrict.gov.uk

NOTES

NOTES

NOTES

NOTES

NOTES

NOTES

LISTING OF CICERONE GUIDES

The Robert Louis Stevenson
Trail
Tour of the Oisans: The GR54
Tour of the Queyras
Tour of the Vanoise
Trekking in the Vosges and Jura
Vanoise Ski Touring
Walking in Provence
Walking in the Cathar Region
Walking in the Cevennes
Walking in the Dordogne
Walking in the Haute Savoie
North & South
Walking in the Languedoc
Walking in the Tarentaise and
Beaufortain Alps
Walking on Corsica

GERMANY
Germany's Romantic Road
Walking in the Bavarian Alps
Walking in the Harz Mountains
Walking the River Rhine Trail

HIMALAYA
Annapurna: A Trekker's Guide
Bhutan
Everest: A Trekker's Guide
Garhwal and Kumaon: A
Trekker's and Visitor's Guide
Kangchenjunga: A Trekker's
Guide
Langtang with Gosainkund and
Helambu: A Trekker's Guide
Manaslu: A Trekker's Guide
The Mount Kailash Trek

IRELAND
Irish Coastal Walks
The Irish Coast to Coast Walk
The Mountains of Ireland

ITALY
Gran Paradiso
Italy's Sibillini National Park
Shorter Walks in the Dolomites
Through the Italian Alps
Trekking in the Apennines
Trekking in the Dolomites
Via Ferratas of the Italian
Dolomites: Vols 1 & 2
Walking in Abruzzo
Walking in Sardinia

Walking in Sicily
Walking in the Central Italian
Alps
Walking in the Dolomites
Walking in Tuscany
Walking on the Amalfi Coast

MEDITERRANEAN
Jordan – Walks, Treks, Caves,
Climbs and Canyons
The Ala Dag
The High Mountains of Crete
The Mountains of Greece
Treks and Climbs in Wadi
Rum, Jordan
Walking in Malta
Western Crete

NORTH AMERICA
British Columbia
The Grand Canyon
The John Muir Trail
The Pacific Crest Trail

SOUTH AMERICA
Aconcagua and the Southern
Andes
Hiking and Biking Peru's Inca
Trails
Torres del Paine

SCANDINAVIA
Trekking in Greenland
Walking in Norway

SLOVENIA, CROATIA AND
MONTENEGRO
The Julian Alps of Slovenia
The Mountains of Montenegro
Trekking in Slovenia
Walking in Croatia

SPAIN AND PORTUGAL
Costa Blanca Walks
1 West & 2 East
Mountain Walking in Southern
Catalunya
The Mountains of Central Spain
Trekking through Mallorca
Walking in Madeira
Walking in Mallorca
Walking in the Algarve
Walking in the Canary Islands
2 East

Walking in the Cordillera
Cantabrica
Walking in the Sierra Nevada
Walking on La Gomera and
El Hierro
Walking on La Palma
Walking on Tenerife
Walking the GR7 in Andalucia
Walks and Climbs in the Picos
de Europa

SWITZERLAND
Alpine Pass Route
Central Switzerland
The Bernese Alps
The Swiss Alps
Tour of the Jungfrau Region
Walking in the Valais
Walking in Ticino
Walks in the Engadine

TECHNIQUES
Geocaching in the UK
Indoor Climbing
Lightweight Camping
Map and Compass
Mountain Weather
Moveable Feasts
Outdoor Photography
Rock Climbing
Sport Climbing
The Book of the Bivvy
The Hillwalker's Guide to
Mountaineering
The Hillwalker's Manual

MINI GUIDES
Avalanche!
Navigating with a GPS
Navigation
Pocket First Aid and Wilderness
Medicine
Snow

For full information on all
our guides, and to order
books and eBooks, visit our
website:
www.cicerone.co.uk.

Walking – Trekking – Mountaineering – Climbing – Cycling

Over 40 years, Cicerone have built up an outstanding collection of 300 guides, inspiring all sorts of amazing adventures.

Every guide comes from extensive exploration and research by our expert authors, all with a passion for their subjects. They are frequently praised, endorsed and used by clubs, instructors and outdoor organisations.

All our titles can now be bought as **e-books** and many as iPad and Kindle files and we will continue to make all our guides available for these and many other devices.

Our website shows any **new information** we've received since a book was published. Please do let us know if you find anything has changed, so that we can pass on the latest details. On our **website** you'll also find some great ideas and lots of information, including sample chapters, contents lists, reviews, articles and a photo gallery.

It's easy to keep in touch with what's going on at Cicerone, by getting our monthly **free e-newsletter**, which is full of offers, competitions, up-to-date information and topical articles. You can subscribe on our home page and also follow us on **Facebook** and **Twitter**, as well as our **blog**.

Cicerone – the very best guides for exploring the world.

CICERONE

2 Police Square Milnthorpe Cumbria LA7 7PY
Tel: 015395 62069 info@cicerone.co.uk
www.cicerone.co.uk